# Blazing Star

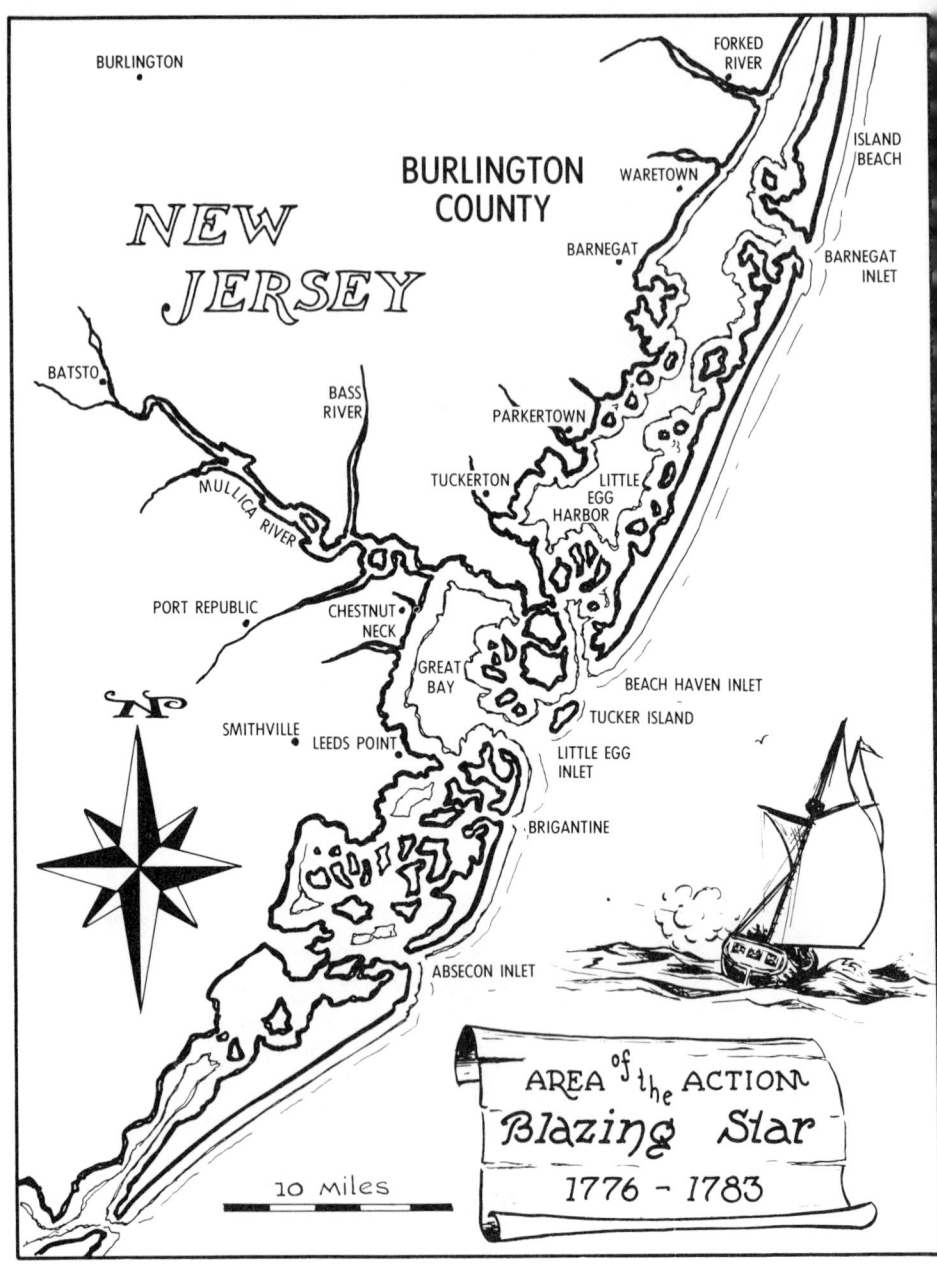

# *Blazing Star*

A Documentary Account of a Small Privateer
During the American Revolution

*C. Malcolm B. Gilman*

South Brunswick and New York: A. S. Barnes and Company
London: Thomas Yoseloff Ltd

*Barry University Library*
*Miami, FL* 33161

© 1974 by A. S. Barnes and Co., Inc.

A. S. Barnes and Co., Inc.
Cranbury, New Jersey 08512

Thomas Yoseloff Ltd
108 New Bond Street
London W1Y OQX, England

Library of Congress Cataloging in Publication Data
Gilman, C          Malcolm B
    Blazing Star; a documentary account of a small privateer during the American Revolution.
    Bibliography: p.
    I. Title.
PZ4.G485B1   [PS3557.I42]          813'.5'4          72-5188
ISBN 0-498-01220-4

OTHER BOOKS BY C. MALCOLM B. GILMAN:

The Story of the Jersey Blues
The Huguenot Migration
Monmouth Road to Glory

PRINTED IN THE UNITED STATES OF AMERICA

Dedicated to my grandchildren

*Lucinda Day Gilman*
*Nicholas Peter Gilman*
*Donald Mark LaFountain*
*Tyler Anne Gilman*
*Daphne Hunter LaFountain*
*Darcy Haines LaFountain*
*Charles Malcolm B. Gilman III*
*David Ayres Gilman*
*Laurence Harvey Gilman*
*Richard Roger Gilman*
*Georgia Jane Gilman*

and to all born and yet unborn children who will strive to defend our country under any and all circumstances.

*Perth Amboy in 1775 (from an old print).*

# INTRODUCTION

The *Blazing Star* was built in 1765 at the little hamlet of Blazing Star on Staten Island Sound, near what is today Sewaren, New Jersey. From the day of its first launching, this trim topsail schooner seemed destined for glory, for as she slipped silently into the waters of Staten Island Sound, she carried a starboard list.

At first this little ship carried furniture between the ports of the colonies. In Rahway, there was a famous cabinet maker named Springer, and in Perth Amboy there was Hunter. There also were three in Elizabethtown, including a famous clock maker by the name of Brokaw, as well as several clock makers in Monmouth. As the restrictions piled up on the Crown Colonies after 1765, the little ship became engaged in contraband and smuggling. It smuggled applejack out of Rahway and Woodbridge; it smuggled tobacco up from Virginia; it smuggled powder the length of the Colonies, locks for arms, gun barrels, cutlasses, books and pamphlets. With the Stamp Act and the closure of the ports, it smuggled tea, glass, paper, cloth, and even men hunted by the Crown.

The name *Blazing Star* soon became a word on the lips of every patriot in the surrounding countryside. There wasn't an inlet along the coastline of the thirteen colonies that she couldn't enter, for her total draft loaded was less than five feet. Her bow was sleek, her canvas trim, and her transom as beautiful as a maiden bathing in the morning sun. She had a comfortable forward cabin for the crew and a beautiful cabin aft for the captain and his mates. Her keel was made from the heart of oak and her planking the finest straight-grained hard pine. Her frames were of oak and the beautiful hand-rubbed paneling of her wardroom consisted of spruce, chestnut and walnut. Her beams across the wardroom cabin top were beautiful hand-rubbed walnut, and her sails had been made by the wives of crew members. She was as comfortable as a plump wife on a cold winter night, and to sail her was a sailor's dream.

And so, when the honorable George Washington stopped at the Rahway Tavern on his way through to take command of the army at Cambridge, these men offered their services and *Blazing Star* was destined to go forth as a privateer, making her place in history, bathed in blood and drenched in fire throughout the American Revolution.

And so our story begins on a beautiful April day in the year of Our Lord 1775, with our trim coastwise schooner lying at its dock along the marsh-lined creek just north of Perth Amboy.

*Blazing Star.*

# Blazing Star

# CREW OF THE *Blazing Star*

| | |
|---|---|
| Robert Hunter | *Captain and Owner* |
| John Hunter | *Mate* |
| Fred Sykes | *Mate* |
| Lewis R. Pearsall | *Mate* |
| William Purchase | *Ships Carpenter and Cabinetmaker* |
| | |
| Howard Hulse | *Rigger, Gunner, Sailor* |
| Henry Springer | *Finisher and Sailor* |
| Louis Springer | *Ships Carpenter and Sailor* |
| Walter Springer | *Sailor and Carpenter* |
| Ed. Hance | *Gunner and Sailor* |
| Cornelius Orange | *Gunner and Sailor* |
| Cornelius Irons | *Gunner and Sailor* |
| Howard Toms | *Gunner and Sailor* |
| Ed. Cook | *Sharpshooter* |
| Alexander Hunter | *Sharpshooter and Apprentice Seaman* |
| | |
| Josiah Drake | *Cabin Boy* |
| Richard Brown | *Cook and Gunner* |

# THE CRY OF CHESTNUT NECK

Today I stood upon the beach along Great Mullica Bay.
I saw a hundred privateers straining as they lay.
There were Brigantines and Barkentines, and little Brigs
  and Barques.
And in the marshland over there I heard the meadow lark.

While in the town, the builder's hammer, sounded new
  construction.
Houses new and shipyards new, and docks for public auction.
A Schooner lay at the dockside, unloading a British prize,
And ladies fair, while Gentlemen stare, which is a
  Gentleman's custom.

There are silks, brocades and lace and guns,
And parasols and silver, and harness stock and powder
  barrels,
And flour from the miller.
While on the cobbled busy streets the drover drives the
  cattle,
And coaches, carriages are in, and all is rush and rattle.
For today the auctioneer will sell to all the highest
  bidders,
The prizes from the British ships while Tory hearts are
  bitter.

And now I hear a thousand sails making for departure,
The squeak of rusty pulleys, above the bid and Barker.
The chant of a thousand sailormen upon the sand strewn decks,
For hopes are high, the picking's good,

>The word is out,
>The tide is right,
>The British ship,
>The "Martin Beck"
>Is off the coast tonight!

Then with a start I looked about,
The squeaking pulleys on making sail are only the bittern's quarrelsome screech,
The gray gulls restless cry in flight.
The shuffling feet of tired men upon the sand strewn deck,
Is only the rhythmic beat of ageless waves upon the sandy beach.

From Tuckertown to Chestnut Neck, and on to Port Republic,
The town is gone, all, all is gone.
The ladies full, in silken dress with buffoon sleeves and parasol,
And tiny steps.

Yes, all is gone, except the deer, the coon, the snake, the bear,
The marshland Hen, the haunts of men,
Complete decay.

>The Lord doth give,
>The Lord shall take away.

# 1

*The first person* to arrive at the dock was Captain Hunter. Sitting beside his lovely wife, he pulled up in a two-wheeled gig with the top down. After a warm good-bye, he stepped briskly down from the carriage, a small leather trunk in one hand, and went aboard without so much as looking back. The carriage, drawn by a beautiful bay gelding of sixteen and a half hands, turned sharply and the horse started off at a fast gallop. The captain was met by his loyal black man, Richard, who carried his trunk to the wardroom under the poop deck.

The next person to arrive was Henry Springer, who drew up in a light, racy high two-wheeled gig, seated beside his young, beautiful, but slightly plump wife. Their embrace was perhaps a little more passionate, realizing too well how long they might be separated. He dismounted, patted the horse affectionately, then energetically mounted the deck and disappeared in the forward cabin. The rest of the crew came on in short order. Fred Sykes, a man of at least 65 years, came all the way from Cranesford and must have walked all the way down to the wharf from the upper end of town; since the stageline ended at the old hotel up on the hill.

Not far away, one of the King's dragoons rode back and forth, so nothing very much was said until the last man had come aboard and they were all gathered in the wardroom. The first man to speak was Captain Hunter.

"Men, we'll sail up to the mouth of the Rahway River and there take aboard the brass gun which was cast at the old foundry on Main Street. All through this region we'll be in healthy territory—just so long as we stay away from the Staten Island side. We have letters of clearance from the Royal Governor, William Franklin, that we're going through to Haverstraw Bay to bring down a load of bricks." We all smiled. "So, I anticipate no trouble unless we're boarded by the British and one of them enters the wardroom and sees the gun. When you go on deck, be calm. Show no excitement or haste. We'll simply sail as we always have, in spite of the fact that we're leaving our homes and an enemy port. It makes me sad to think that Perth Amboy is in British hands."

The men sauntered lazily onto the deck, talking and gossiping as though they had a leisurely day ahead of them. As they walked about the boat, the jib was finally hoisted, the two mainsails run up, and the lines cast off. Then we set the outer jib and we were off, glad to be away from that dock. We were on our way into the future, into a great unknown.

We sailed up the sound toward the Rahway River on a typical, southerly April breeze. Richard appeared on deck with an old banjo and began to play. Some of the words he sang were unintelligible, but the music was beautiful. The water lapped along the streak and under the bow and the water trickled out in its regular triangular pattern astern.

The marshy lowlands on the Jersey side of the sound were taking on their late April green. The willows, particularly the swamp willows along Staten Island on the edges of the farms, were showing the slightest tinge of yellow. The fat cows and unclipped well-rounded sheep stood silently in the pastures or munched at the new spring grass. What a beautiful afternoon!

It wasn't long before the mouth of the Rahway River stood ahead. We were arriving too early to pick up the cannon; it was still quite light out. So we slackened sail, drifted along more slowly and enjoyed our pipes. Richard continued to play his banjo and this sail was as close to paradise as I ever hope to get.

No matter how much we tried to cut down our speed, the *Blazing Star* seemed to race along at a fast clip. Soon we reached the Rahway River, jibed and started up. We had to go about a mile and a half to Henry Springer's farm, where we would pick up our brass ten-pounder. The river was not more than two hundred feet wide, but it was fairly deep and on a south wind, so that even though we slackened sail, we arrived at Springer's farm well before dark.

He wanted to avoid an atmosphere of mystery or suspicion, so when we stepped from the schooner, it was agreed that we would all say good-bye and go off in different directions, as though we were going home. At night, we would then gather and complete our job. Henry, of course, went into his house; Captain Robert followed. The rest of us went off in several directions until we came to the woods, where we sat down and waited. After dark we saw our signal—a light in the farmhouse. We immediately went to the barn and wheeled out our little ten-pounder. This was no small job, for it must have weighed five or six hundred pounds, but it was beautifully done. It bore the mark, insignia, and date of casting at the Rahway foundry, for its makers were proud of their job, no matter what it might cost them if this gun fell into British hands. Fortunately, it never did.

We loaded the gun aboard and placed it in the wardroom. Then Henry Springer had a fine idea. "Let's build a bed for the captain on this side of the wardroom. We can make it in such a way that it fits into the paneling, but can be slid out and lifted up—and when the gun is not in use, we'll hide it under the bed." This was indeed a clever idea and I'm sure that it put us beyond suspicion more than once.

We tried to time this trip so we would be on our way before Henry's wife returned from Perth Amboy, where she had taken her husband. The drive from Perth Amboy down to the farm along the Rahway River, below the Lees Town Bridge, was almost fifteen miles, and we knew it would be well after dark before she returned. We didn't want her to know anything about the gun or our visit, in case she were ever questioned by Loyalists or Tories. We were taking the same precautions with our crew's wives; we told them nothing.

We sailed down the Rahway River close hauled, for we were still on the south wind. The evening was a grand one, and once or twice slight banks of fog collected and dissipated, because the air was warm and the water cold. When we reached the sound, we turned upward toward the port of Elizabethtown. All along here we were in friendly hands; a Tory or Loyalist had no place here since long ago they had fled to Staten Island.

We sailed throughout the evening up past Elizabethtown and on into the bay below the marshes of Newark, where we decided to remain for the night. We had yet to build the famous stowaway bed designed to cover our beautiful, brass, stern gun. The smell of tea, country bacon and eggs was beginning to emerge from the galley and the great question was who would take the wheel. It was soon settled by Captain Hunter, for he ordered her about and to stand in stays, and he told Richard to drop the hook. The sails came down and we hung our anchor light out, since we were well beyond the sight of the enemy.

We filed down through the companionway and sat at the table with our backs against the wall. The galley was small; it would hold only six men, two at each side and one at each end of the table, while Richard sat at the side on his home-made high-back barrel chair. After a good meal, we settled back and the conversation drifted to our great general. What a fine man the general was and how much dignity he had!

When Captain Hunter passed around the tobacco bowl, he did not forget to turn and pass it to Richard, who took his share with a smile. Richard had an old homemade pipe made from applewood, which smoked just as well as our long, clay, church wardens, perhaps even better. We sat throughout the evening, first in the galley drinking tea and then in the captain's cabin, discussing the stirring events of the last ten years. Things had moved rapidly since the French and Indian Wars, and from 1765 to 1775 the situation had gradually become more desperate—although the Crown was still trying to pacify us without appearing to give in. The attitude of the

Barrel Chair

The Main Cabin, The Captain's Quarters

dragoon on the road behind the dock was one of warm friendliness. He could have come over and asked to see our papers, but undoubtedly he had been told not to meddle or interfere.

After a while our captain pulled out his watch and said, "Boys, I think we'd better turn in. I don't think the tide will be favorable. If we get the wrong wind, we'll have a beat up Kill Von Kull and possibly a head wind into New York. We want to get an early start in the morning."

I was awakened in the morning by Richard's singing as he scrubbed down the deck. I dressed hurriedly and appeared on deck, where I found the captain was already there, looking everything over as carefully as though she'd just been rigged. As the men appeared, he spoke to each in turn. How he was able to predict the weather I don't know, but the wind was east and it meant a beat up Kill Von Kull all right. Without delay we hauled the hook, dipped it a few times to free it of the mud, and set sail. We cleared the rocks at a safe distance at the entrance to Newark Bay and proceeded on to New York.

We ate breakfast in relays, for it was necessary to maintain one man at the wheel and three on the sails. The tacks were short, troublesome, and slow, and the tide was beginning to set against us. Within half a day we had reached the upper bay, then we headed almost on the quarter and raced for New York town.

What a cut-water this little ship had! It was like a dream. As I stared under her bowsprit down along the chain at her fullness forward, I became a little homesick. How long would I be away? Would I ever see my home again? But I cast this all aside, for now I must be a man, and my thoughts drifted back to the ship. She fairly slid over the water, which seemed to rush beneath and lift her even more. She was ten years old and never had been beaten in a coastwise merchantmen's race. She had quite a reputation along the seaboard. Men said she was enchanted, a sailor's dream.

By the time we put in to the dock at New York, Henry Springer, with some help from Richard, had finished the beautiful built-in bunk. The cannon was no longer in sight and a good walnut stain made from the green hulls of walnuts had been rubbed into the wood, followed by tallow, fat and bee's wax. They had rubbed and rubbed until there was no difference in the appearance of the paneling beneath the new bunk and the paneling along the rest of the wall. It was really a fine piece of cabinet work. I had just enough time to examine this beautiful bunk when I heard the captain call, "All hands on deck!" I fairly flew up the companionway and, as I jumped to my position, the captain smiled. "Nice job, don't you think?"

"Very nice, Captain. Looks as if it might have originally been built into the ship."

The captain nodded and waved his hand to slacken off sail. We now turned into the wind and slid up along the dock as gracefully as a beautiful lady slides her trim foot into a sequined slipper. We were now in New York, a town of Tories, Rebels, Loyalists, indifferent Quakers, and foreigners from all corners of the world, each with their own opinions on politics, love, business, and women. As we arrived, the old New York militia regiment was training on the Bowling Green, and many people stood on the docks to watch, admiring our trim little ship as we pulled in.

David Ayres[1] of Woodbridge, major of the New Jersey Scout Rangers Battalion came down and had a conference with our captain. We were all glad to see him and after the conference, he sat around on the deck admiring the ship and remarked that some day he hoped to own one just like it. After he left, we were called into the main saloon and Captain Hunter told us our new detail.

There was powder stored in a warehouse near Peekskill, and we were to sail up and get it. This was a stroke of luck, for it would explain our trip to Haverstraw for any inquisitive eyes. That evening we walked about the town, looking into the pubs. Finally we all went over to Fraunces, had a tankard of ale, and then came back and went to bed. Early in the morning, with a southeast breeze and a fair tide, we hoisted sail and started up the beautiful Hudson River, with the low marshes of Paulus Hook to the west, the Palisades ahead to the left, and the snug town of New York on our right.

We could see the water carts already on the streets, selling fresh water by the pail; it was a busy little place. The militia was again training on the Green, and oddly enough the small British garrison which had been stationed in New York departed after Bunker Hill. It was evident that this garrison wanted no experience like the one in Boston. We later heard that it had gone across to Staten Island and from there joined the garrison at Perth Amboy.

As we sailed up the river, Henry Springer continued to finish the beautiful panel base of the built-in poster completing cunning disguise. By sliding out the panels, the gun could be rolled out and we began to practice with it. We rolled the gun into position, although we never opened the stern window when it was out, and went through the actions of loading and firing. Of course, we didn't actually load. An alarm would be sounded, the gunners would grab the gun and secure it under the bed, then replace the paneling. From Captain Hunter's standpoint, the only bad feature was that the ball and kegs of powder were stored under his bed.

It was another beautiful day without a cloud in the sky. As we approached the Harlem River, the current, caused by a change in the tide, was rushing over the rocks and down over the rapids. The trees on the shore were beginning to burst their buds and the trim little town of Harlem stood out on the side of the hill. We swept on past the Harlem, for the lower land now allowed the wind to fill our sails more completely. Soon Yonkers was up ahead, the Palisades were beginning to fall away on the west, and the smell of the river mixed with that of the land was invigorating to us all.

Yonkers was a pretty little town with two fine schooners standing at the beach, very close in, their anchors down. We sailed on past Tarrytown on Haverstraw Bay, and soon we were entering the Tappan Zee, an inland sea where the river is about two miles wide and opens into a beautiful bay. (It was here that Henry Hudson thought he had discovered a passageway into the Pacific Ocean.) The brickyards at

Haverstraw were in operation, but we were not interested in brick and sailed on past. The mountains were on the west side now and the hills of Ossining on the east; as far up as we could see were the highlands of the Hudson. Here the river seemed to end abruptly with mountains all around, but this was only because up ahead, far above Peekskill, the river made a sharp S-curve to the west and then proceeded again northward at West Point. We were approaching our destination and could soon see the little town nestled on the side of the hill on the east bank.

"We're making very good time, Captain."

"Yes, my boy. Will you take over the wheel for a spell?"

"Aye, aye, sir!"

In Peekskill Bay the view was beautiful. The fish were jumping and the gulls were soaring lazily. The clouds hung like hammocks in the sky. This was another of the pretty Hudson River towns. Just as soon as we tied up, I was relieved at the wheel and then I saw the powder on the dock. As I'd never been in Peekskill before, I jumped ashore and made a quick tour of the town.

Many of the houses were of brick, because there was at least one brickyard down near Verplank's Ferry. The houses were in neat rows and there was a fine, large stone house being built on a bluff. From its layout and detail I could tell that the owner was obviously of considerable wealth. Here was a man who was gambling on there being no war. The central portion of the house was of the hard traprock stone of the Hudson Valley. The wings on either side were connected by brick passageways based very much on the current style of English manor houses. The roof was not yet placed, but the rough floors were in and the fireplaces were finished except for the mantels.

I took one long look across the river. It was breathtaking. Row after row of lovely mountains, like great waves one behind the other, spread out before my eyes. The view down the river as far as I could see, and up at least as far as the island in front of the long sprawling Bear Mountain (so named by the Indians because it resembled a sleeping bear)

Dutch Gnow and Row Galley.

*Shallop, an open boat propelled by oar or sail. Often a whale boat.*

was arresting. Then I ran all the way down the hill back to the dock, for I had taken too much time.

The crew had just finished loading the last cask of powder and everyone was enjoying a tankard of hard cider as I jumped aboard. Apparently I had been little missed. A tankard was passed to me and although I consumed it with ease, I soon felt its effect. The captain took his place at the wheel, and nodded for the sails to go up; with another nod the lines were cast off. We waved good-bye to our compatriots, jibed the *Blazing Star*, and started down the river.

The powder casks were small but we spent much time trying to decide how to hide them. We couldn't construct a false bottom in the ship, for in the event of a leak all the powder would be destroyed. Also, below a false bottom the powder would become damp. It was finally decided that we would hide the powder forward hidden by our extra canvas, rope, marlin and other ship supplies.

There was quite a bit of traffic on this river. We passed many large row boats, or row galleys, often manned by as many as twenty slaves. The masts were stuck up forward so they would sail under a favorable wind. We passed several sloops and shallops, and occasionally a brig or a brigantine. As we again reached the Harlem, we saw several barks and many more schooners, for schooners were now beginning to be very popular.* The ones I saw were the two or three mast variety, very maneuverable and quick to go about; with the coming in of the clipper bow at this time, they were very fast. All of those sailing in our direction were easily overtaken, however, and all those which had left port after us had fallen further and further behind, for our little ship had always been exceedingly fast, unusually seaworthy and comfortable.

We sailed on down the river into the setting sun and with it came the death of the wind. We drifted over along the Jersey shore and threw out the hook, for the tide was now

---

*This name originated in Gloucester, Massachusetts, in 1739. "See how she schoons!"

unfavorable. A great many of the other little boats did likewise. Thus came a rendezvous for ships.

We "spoke" several ships, but were not too cordial because we did not want anyone aboard. We had to think up a story in case we were intercepted and asked what we had done with our bricks. But then we recalled that this was not likely because the British garrison had left New York and was now on Staten Island. But we thought it better to be prepared, for they might send a shallop or a sloop up the river to keep an eye on traffic and to watch for smugglers. We hung out our stern light and anchor light on the bow and went below for a good dinner. Richard had gotten up an excellent meal. He was now accustomed to sailing in smooth water, but he had some terrifying experiences ahead of him—boiling inlets, mountainous breakers, dangerous shoals, alarming storms, high winds and moaning rigging. He would spend many nights in a lonesome bunk, listening in the dark to the creaking of the ship.

I understood Richard's fear of rough water very well. The first time I passed through an inlet between the bars through the huge, roaring, crashing breakers, I was certain it would be my last, for we would be swamped. But as we approached the first breaker and the bow of the *Blazing Star* lifted and the breaker parted and raced on astern, I was satisfied, I would have no further fear. Richard was yet to have his first experience with all these things.

# 2

*After a hearty* evening meal, we all went on deck. The older members of the crew sat about spinning yarns and smoking their pipes. I sat off to one side, as a boy should, and admired the lovely evening. The twinkling of the stars and the blinking of the lights, especially the anchor lights on the ships around us, added to the enchantment. In a short while the men turned in and I was left alone. I was beginning to feel just a little homesick and I thought how silly it was, since I was such a short distance from home. I could swim ashore, hitch my way on almost any cart, and be home in a matter of two days. And so I talked myself out of my homesickness, for I realized that in the future I might be a long, long way from home. For centuries boys had been away from home and not as well off as I. How foolish even to think about being homesick! I went to bed.

  We arose early on the morrow and sailed with a favorable wind and a slack tide to the town dock at the end of the island in front of the redoubt and the fort. New York was an active town and everyone seemed busy. Bonneted women were carrying their market baskets and small children were rolling their hoops.

  Watercart men were selling water by the bucket, men were working on houses, and home merchandise was being unloaded and reloaded onto river vessels.

On the 23rd of April, 1775, the day after the dissolution of the Provincial Congress of New York, the news from Lexington burst upon us. Though it was Sunday, two sloops which lay at our wharf laden with flour and supplies for the British at Boston, valued at eight thousand pounds, were speedily unloaded. Isaac Sears joined with John Lamb to stop all vessels going to Quebec, Newfoundland, Georgia or Boston, where British authority was still in control. Now we all carried our arms publicly and even I, with my pistol in my belt, and my bandana tied stoutly at the back of my head, paraded about the dock with the others. The people assembled at a drum beat and the customs house was shut. The merchants whose vessels had been cleared, dared not let them sail.

The shock and horror because of Lexington and Concord became more and more impressive as people drifted in daily from parts of New England and most particularly from Boston. Darkness had closed upon the country. Men on horseback were riding up and down the length and breadth of the land, even to the farthest frontier settlements and to Canada, especially to Quebec and Montreal. Little did we believe that when Gage left New York "to put the rebel hordes down forever" that he would perpetrate what he did at Lexington and Concord.

The following days they took the military stores from New York. Volunteer companies were now parading in the streets and on the Green. All cannon were hauled from the city to Kingsbridge for safekeeping at the north end of the island. Church of England men, Jews, Catholics and Presbyterians took up arms and marched side by side. The "Old Committee of 51," because it lagged behind the changing conditions, was replaced by a committee of one hundred, resolved in the most emphatic manner to stand or fall with "our continent."

Although this committee knew, at the time, that there were not five hundred pounds of powder in the city, they sent a demanding letter to the King ordering several regiments to be removed from New York and commanded Brooklyn Heights to be fortified, although they knew the deep water of the harbor exposed it to ships of war on both sides.

The packet for England had hardly passed Sandy Hook when, on the sixth, the delegates to the First Continental Congress (at Philadelphia) from Massachusetts and Connecticut came in. Three miles from the city they were met by a company of grenadiers led by David Ayres, our neighbor, and a regiment of militia under arms (the Jersey Blues). They were followed by a cavalcade of carriages and many thousands of people on foot. The roads were crowded as if the whole city had come to meet them and they made their entry amidst loud acclamations, the ringing of bells, and joyful demonstrations. How we wished to fire our brass gun, but we didn't.

The delegation from Massachusetts became a part of New York. They were escorted across the Hudson River by two hundred militia under arms, and triumphs still awaited them at Newark and Elizabeth. Royal Governor Franklin of New Jersey could not conceal his chagrin that Gage had risked commencing hostilities while peace was being negotiated.

A courier came in on the 18th of May and told of Arnold's success at St. Johns and the capture of Ticonderoga and Crown Point. A schooner called the *Liberty* had been manned, armed and commanded by Benedict Arnold, who had had much experience at sea. With a fresh southerly wind, he readily passed Lake Champlain and on that day, with a party in boats, he surprised a sergeant and twelve men, captured their arms, two serviceable brass field pieces, and a British sloop which lay in St. Johns harbor. In about an hour the wind shifted in his favor and, with his prisoners and prizes, he sailed home.

On the 11th of June, the Provincial Congress of Massachusetts proposed to extend hostilities to the sea. The subject was introduced, but it was so difficult for the colony to conceive itself in a state of war with Great Britain, the decision was continually postponed in the hope of a return of the peace. "A war has begun," wrote Joseph Warren, a member of the Massachusetts Congress, "but I hope after a full conviction both of our ability and resolution to maintain our right, that Britain will act with necessary wisdom. This I most heartily wish as I feel a warm affection still for the parent state." This was the reason that, with couriers arriving daily from all parts of the colonies and with proclamation after proclamation going up on the boards about the town, we were still immobile, for we had not yet been given the authority or orders to go forth and harass the coastal commerce of the British. The captain said, "We are a ship without a fair wind."

Things were happening fast. There was so much news coming in and out of New York, and the town crier's bell called us so often to the Green to receive official news, we scarcely had time to do any work aboard ship. However, we took enough time to keep her in Bristol fashion.[2]

The first important decision of Congress pertained to New York. On the fifteenth, the city and county asked how to conduct their affairs regarding the British regiments, known to be under orders to occupy that place. With the sanction of John Jay and his colleagues in Philadelphia, they were instructed "not to oppose the landing of the troops, but not to suffer them to erect fortifications; to act on the defensive, but only for the protection of the inhabitants, their property and to repel force by force."

Our captain had been waiting a long time for word from Congress. He was just as up in the air now as he had been before, for it still gave him no sanction whatsoever to fight. Many of the men from ships along the docks were talking of becoming privateers, but without a government and with no letters of mark, they didn't dare. If captured, we would be strung up on the yardarm as pirates. To make matters worse, the Continental Congress itself was embarrassed. It recognized the existing Royal Government of New York and tolerated its Governor Tryon and all the naval and military officers, contractors and Indian agents in the peaceful discharge of their functions. In evidence of this, we saw the British vessel of war, the Asia, supplied with provisions from land, yet she was restrained in any traffic from ship to shore. The entire situation was embarrassing and constricting.

Although there was tremendous individual enthusiasm on the part of the committees and the volunteers, there was still a great lack of concerted and planned effort. This, as well as inadequate individual leadership, was causing the men to fall away from enlisting both in New York and Boston, like the withering of unplucked grapes on a vine.

Day after day we sat aboard ship, fearful that one of the two British frigates in the harbor might decide to search all the American coastwise sailors—or even to impound them. We knew well that if we were searched we would be taken prisoners. We longed for home at such a short distance away and yet we were afraid. Although it was only a day's sail, the Crown Colony at Perth Amboy might very suddenly impound our schooner and imprison us. Things were moving fast. The British garrisons on Staten Island and the sloops and shallops, the frigates and transports in Raritan and New York Bay were patrolling the waters around New York.

Our captain had been corresponding regularly with the New York committee, but to no avail. They had no authority, and their hope was still that reconciliation would take place; they hesitated to offend the Crown. Captain Hunter next corresponded with the New Jersey committee, but with no results. And when the Massachusetts and Connecticut representatives arrived in New York on their way to the Continental Congress, he met them and offered his service, but none had the power to commission or authorize him, and most certainly none of them would put anything in writing. And so our captain returned from these meetings discouraged, downhearted, dejected and apprehensive for his country's safety and its future. Our lack of leadership was so appalling that the British were counting on this to help them put down the King's rebellious subjects.

On Sunday, the 20th of June, it happened. It was a beautiful morning. The Church bells of Trinity and St. Paul's, the chapel of Kings College, were pealing almost like a funeral toll. Perhaps the sexton was putting the proper feeling of the times into his work. The fruit trees were blooming in all their glory. They were very late that year because the spring had been so cool. The birds were singing happily and even the gulls seemed to have found a more pleasant tune. The pastures were a lovely waving green and there were no cattle, for they had long since been sent to Kingsbridge. I was in the water and the men were sitting about the deck, talking, smoking, or fishing. Richard was reading his Bible.

Suddenly the captain noticed a sloop flying a British ensign, sailing straight for the dock. "I wonder what they want," said the captain. "They agreed not to land." I came out of the water and we all watched the sloop. As she drew near, we could see that she was manned by men from the Perth Amboy Garrison. We hailed them by a wave of the hat or hand, but they made no reply.

They tied up at the dock, although by all rights they were not supposed to do so, for they had been instructed not to come ashore. There were 36 men, including the officers, who then formed on the dock and marched straight to our little ship. Not one of our men spoke. Their captain, with all pomp and ritual came aboard, followed by half the platoon. He walked directly up to Captain Hunter and addressed him haughtily. "Are you the captain of this ark?"

"I am," said the captain with a smile. None of us had ever seen such self-control.

"I will see your papers."

"I'll see you in hell," mumbled someone.

"Fetch our papers, boy," said the captain to Josiah Drake. "Yes, sir, Captain." The boy disappeared down the hatch. We stared at the British soldiers and sailors as they stood at attention, never moving a muscle. Their captain tried to appear bored as he "pinched" his snuff. Our captain later said he thought he was frightened. The papers were brought and the Britisher examined them, apparently looking for some loophole. Finally, as he returned them to Captain Hunter, he spoke.

"Went to Haverstraw for a load of bricks?" With that he touched a pinch of snuff to either side of his nostril, applied his lace handkerchief, looked about the boat as though he were looking for the bricks and then exclaimed, "And where are these bricks?"

Only once in a lifetime do I ever get a smart thought, but I got one then. "Please, sir," I said, "we sold them to a man in Peekskill by the name of Young, who is building a fine house on the bluff overlooking the bay—a stone house with brick wings."

He looked at me in scorn, turned away, then turned back to me. "Yes," he said. "You are a child and will probably be the only one of these farmers who would tell the truth." He placed his hand on my shoulder and continued. "You know Governor Franklin, my boy. You wouldn't lie to him now, would you?"

"Governor Franklin has spoken to me and waved to me many times," I said. "And besides, my grandfather was governor of the Province of East Jersey in 1702." That seemed to spike his gun and he asked no more questions.

He turned to our captain. "You will return to Perth Amboy with all haste. If things continue," he looked about the ship again, "you will join His Majesty's service." He ordered the soldiers turned, and in a column of stiff two's descended to the dock. The Britisher followed—but not before Howard Toms spat a quid of tobacco which landed on the tail of his coat. I almost died on the spot. Fortunately, the British captain neither saw nor felt it.

They set sail and I was happy to see them disappear as they turned into Kill Von Kull. For the second time during this episode, the captain smiled. "Boy, that was once where speaking out of turn was worthwhile. Some people say boys should speak only when spoken to." He smiled and patted me on the back. "I say, speak when you have something to say." I felt very proud. I may have prevented prison bars on the Jersey, or even the cord.

The captain continued. "I was just thinking. I intended to tell the limey that the quality of the bricks was such that we wouldn't buy them. Suppose the boy and I had started our tales at the same time? We would all be going down Kill Von Kull now." He laughed heartily, but I didn't, and no one smiled.

Someone suggested a celebration, and the rum and apple was broken out. Richard said, "I think I'll bake a cake for our boy, one with black walnuts." I enjoyed the cake and I

*17*

enjoyed being a hero. My only fear was that they might be back.

On the 25th of June, a courier arrived,* tired, unshaven, disheveled, somewhat ragged and worn, but with high spirit and great excitement. The people soon crowded around him and it was impossible for me to get close. In a short while, the towncrier came along, ringing his bell and announcing, "This evening at the hour of seven, there will be an important meeting at Trinity Church." I followed along to ascertain what this meeting might be about and he turned to me with sternness. "Boy, you smell of the sea and the weather is warm. Begone, you're attracting flies." I must have looked crestfallen, for he immediately stopped, took me by the shoulder and patted me on the back. "You're a fine lad. You be at the church tonight. There's been a great battle and we've had a great success. You'll hear all about it from an eyewitness, a man who took part in it from start to finish." I don't remember whether I thanked him, but I went tearing off in leaps and bounds down the green, ascended the dock and with a leap I landed on the deck of our ship. When I told Captain Hunter what I had heard, he told me I was an alert boy and that I would become a worthy man.

Not by order of the captain, but by friendly discussion among the crew, it was decided that the captain and I should attend the meeting. The captain because he was the representative of us all and I because I might remember more of all that might be said. And so on this memorable evening, the 25th of June, 1775, we walked across the green and up Broadway to Trinity Church. Crowds were coming from all directions and we feared that the church might be filled before we got there.

By seven o'clock the church was filled and our courier, now shaven, his wig powdered, and wearing clean linen and fine clothes which he had undoubtedly borrowed for the occasion, ascended the rostrum and began to tell the valiant tale of the battle of Bunker Hill. Not a soul left during his

---
*Paul Revere.

discourse. Many women cried and a few fainted. Some men forgot that they were in church and softly (and some not so softly) cursed. One old codger left his seat and walked up and down the aisle, shaking his cane, reliving the battle. At another point, another old timer cried out, "Were you scared?" For the first time the congregation smiled. The speaker smiled, too, drank from a silver church beaker, and continued. When he finished, he sat down and the minister waited for some time. The meeting was humble, hushed by the appalling knowledge that so many of our countrymen had been killed. Finally the minister arose and walked to the altar, then turned to us with a faint smile. "Let us pray. Good Lord, deliver us from our enemies, Amen." He turned and walked slowly down through the chancel of the church, then through the nave and on out to the door. The people slowly filed out and a number gathered around the courier.

The captain and I walked quietly down the street and for a long while nothing was said. About the time we crossed the green, he turned to me and said, "Boy, I hope your life will be a long, happy and a prosperous one. You may never hear of a more stirring event than you have this night. Tomorrow we sail. I have a hunch the British fleet will be in New York before long." We boarded our ship and were met by the crew, who were sitting on deck, smoking and anxiously waiting. The captain told the story without one interruption. Occasionally he would turn to me and ask me some little item, which I hope I filled in satisfactorily.

"Men, there is no doubt that in the morning the British ships in the harbor will seize our fleet. Therefore, we must be gone before daybreak. I think the safest route for us to follow is up the sound of Long Island and out around Nantucket, for if we are detected proceeding down the Narrows, we will most certainly be stopped."

"Might I suggest, Captain, that we go down Staten Island Sound, past Perth Amboy and Tottenville, and on out through Raritan Bay, thus avoiding the fleet," said Mr. Sykes.

"I think that might be dangerous. The Crown controls Staten Island, Perth Amboy and the narrow isthmus of land between the two. In view of our orders, allowing us to go to Haverstraw to gather brick, I'm afraid they might fire on us if they see us passing Perth Amboy. Up Long Island Sound and the East River, we stand a good chance all the way out, for we have extremely loyal friends here on both sides of the water." This was a demonstration of the complete thought our captain always gave to details. "I also think it might be a bad thing to sail too close to home. It might just increase our longings, don't you think?" The captain smiled and his smile was infectious. We all smiled and one by one went off to bed.

# 3

*Before daylight I* was routed out of bed by the sailor who had stood the night watch. Presently the entire crew was in motion. The fo'c's'l men came through the hatch and appeared on deck barefooted. Almost simultaneously the officers appeared from the wardroom cabin. I looked out from the companionway; our shrouds could just be seen. There was a faint draft of air astir that early June morning, but there was no sign of light in the sky. The watch lights on the ships at anchor in the harbor could not be seen for the haze. The British frigate which lay alongside No-man's-land (the island opposite and southwest of Governor's Island) could not be distinguished and neither could its riding lights. Without so much as a word, the sails went up slowly and noiselessly. The squeak of the pulleys resembled the quarreling of the gulls. The lines were cast off, and we drifted around the point of the Battery and into the East River under a very light breeze. There was scarcely enough to ripple the water, but it must have been ordained by the Almighty, for it was just what we wanted. The wind was light out of the southwest, exactly what we needed to steer up the East River and through Hell's Gate. Our course lay directly up the river and I, the youngest, and presumably with the best eyes, was placed on the bow to watch lest we run afoul on one of the several rocky uninhabited islands in the river.

The last house of New York was soon left far behind and the beautiful bays along the Brooklyn shore were just beginning to appear. The breeze increased and the fog was lifting. Dawn was breaking. A new day lay ahead, but what was in store for us, only time would tell. The beautiful homes on the farms along these little bays, beyond Brooklyn Heights and the beginning of the major portion of Long Island, could now be seen. From time to time, each of us looked back, not for fear of a pursuer, but longingly because as the ripple increased and our wake lengthened with our speed, we were leaving home farther behind. No one knew if we would ever see it again.

The sun was coming up now, the first golden rays of a beautiful morning. It was warm and the air smelled of the sea. The captain summoned me from the bow watch. All hands were now ordered to stand by, the top sails were ordered up, the outer jib and the flying jib were set, and the yardarm of the foremast was dropped to the deck. I was sent to the fo'c's'l to fetch the fore squaresail and the fore topsail. Each of them was a pretty big order for a boy, although I was a big boy and nearly seventeen. I managed to get the fore main squaresail to the top of the steps and dropped it on the deck, where the men seized it, unrolled it and whipped it to the yardarm. The fore topsail was not as difficult and it was soon serviced. As this great sail was set, we could not only hear the increased lapping of the water, we could feel the increased surge of our little ship. The wind had freshened and daylight was coming on rapidly now.

Hearing a roar of water, I looked ahead, and to my great fear and consternation, it seemed that all I could see were great rocks and rushing, crashing water, tumbling at different levels. We were sailing right into it and I moved back toward Captain Hunter. "Boy," he said, "come up on the poop deck. I want to show you something."

"Yes, sir." This time I did not bound up the steps, for I was too frightened. I backed up slowly, never taking my eyes off the sight ahead. I walked across the poop deck slowly, turned about, and looked ahead again at this roaring, crashing, breaking mass of foam and rock.

"This is Hell's Gate, my son. This is the final burial ground for many a good ship, and many a sound captain and his crew. You will notice that where this water is foaming and churning, there are currents, eddies, and rocks, but as we approach, you will see up close to the Long Island shore a steep rock called Black Rock. It is reputed that there is ninety feet of water there and, therefore, there isn't too much current. Had the wind been unfavorable, we would not go through now, but since it is favorable, it will be like spreading molasses on hot pancakes, and you'll enjoy it just as much." His broad, friendly, infectious smile appeared again and my confidence immediately returned. I smiled, too. Then I swallowed hard, took a deep breath of sea air, reached over and held on to the poop rail. "Boy, come over here and help hold the wheel. Get the feel of this wheel going through Hell's Gate. Get the pull and the tug and you sail her through."

"Yes, sir."

It now appeared that we were heading straight into the rocks. My fear returned and my heart no longer beat in my chest; it was pounding in my throat. But just at the moment when I thought we would surely swing into the rocks, the captain called the men on deck and asked them to stand by the lines. Presently all the men were at their stations and, as he passed the wheel slightly over to starboard, the men took up the slack in the sheets, and the boat veered and heeled only slightly, and sailed off like it was skidding toward Black Rock. Then, just as suddenly, the captain turned the wheel hard over to port and then corrected it, and the wheel spun back so quickly for a second that I cracked my knuckles on the holds. The lines were again corrected and the captain shouted down, "Boys, you corrected them just the right amount." The crew was proud, looked back and smiled. We now were sailing before the wind and going up the sound. Hell's Gate was behind us and we were making fine time.

The sound was opening up and the captain pointed out that the Connecticut shore lay ahead on the northeast side. New York had fallen far behind and the little hamlet of Rye was off to the north, then we saw Port Chester. He pointed out the various bays on the Long Island side as well. This was beautiful country; if we could only continue to sail throughout the war in this kind of country with seas as calm as this, how nice it would be. I was frightened again when I thought of the tales I had heard along the docks during our long sojourn in New York—tales of rebel hangings, of imprisonment and starvation on the *Jersey*, and of British brutality. Soon I heard the beat to breakfast and, not knowing what my duties might be, I did not respond. Mate Sykes relieved me at the wheel. The captain beckoned and preceded me down the companionway. We had the usual fine breakfast and I ate my fill. The captain was a large man, over six feet, and his weight must have been well over two hundred pounds. But he was just as big in heart. His thoughts were always for the comfort of his crew and the care of his little ship.

As we sat about the table after eating, the captain started to talk about plans and then realized that Mr. Sykes was alone up on the deck, so he decided to hold the meeting there. We all adjourned to the deck and sat around while Mr. Sykes steered. What a sailor he was! His name was Fred and he came from Cranesford. He had been a selectman there for a long time, but sailing was his first love and turning an honest dollar was his second. He could turn an honest dollar into two faster than any man I ever knew. He was tall and lean, about 65 years of age and a friend of Captain Hunter. They spoke frankly to each other, but always held the greatest mutual respect and so as Captain Hunter began to talk, he was speaking more to Mr. Sykes than anyone else. "We're going to have to do something about getting more armament. We're small enough, God knows, and so we've got to have more guns, more men, more cannon, and more swivels, and even more muskets."

'If we do that, Captain, we've sure got to have more men."

"That's just the thing that's worrying me, Mr. Sykes. There's a happy medium between the number of men we can carry, the guns we can service, and the amount of provisions we must carry. If we take prisoners, we'll need a certain number of men to guard them. We mustn't be overburdened by men or armament. Men can get in the way and armament means weight. The way I see it, there'll be many times when we'll have to hit and run."

"That's exactly the way I see it, Captain."

These two men were talking and discussing for our benefit. We were all friends in this enterprise. We were not paid hands, but rather we were on this journey for our country, most particularly at the moment to help Massachusetts.

"If we can find a couple of good men, Captain, why not just start off with two; that would give four on watch, and four off."

"I had something like that in mind, Fred. Judging by the rest of the small coastwise boats tied up at New York, that seems about right. Practically all of them are going into privateering, and if fifty percent of the coastwise ships go into privateering, the coastwise ocean will be practically covered by American privateers. That means that only rarely will we operate alone or be a very great distance from another privateer."

And so it was decided that as soon as we rounded the Indian point of Montauk, we would put in at Sagg Harbour and look for sailors. The sound was now opening up, the coast line was falling away on either side and, as we sailed up the middle of the Sound, the shorelines could just be made out. The houses were like tiny toys along the shore. This was beautiful virgin countryside, with the forest stretching down to the beaches. Here and there could be seen clumps of trees and rocky cliffs tumbling into the sound, giving mute evidence of how severe storms can be on this body of water.

It was decided that Herb and three of the other men should now go down and practice on the "ward" gun, as it became known. After they had been gone for a long time, the captain wandered down and was pleasantly surprised by the speed of their delivery.

It was wild country now. Occasionally a small sloop or shallop was the only sign of civilization. I was looking for Indians, for the only Indians I had seen were two lonely ones sitting on a rock at Kipps Bay as we were going up the East River. They looked forlorn and pensive as they sat with their arms braced against their knees, their chins resting on their hands, and they looked as though they might have been sorry they sold Manhattan Island. I wondered if that was what they were thinking. The white man, with his war canoes, had only brought headaches and heartaches to the human race.

We were bouncing along now in a spanking breeze, and there was just enough sea running for her to lift and fall in the most graceful manner, almost like a lovely lady waltzing and swaying in billowing skirts. Mr. Sykes rang the bell to assemble all men on deck. The wind had veered now and was coming out of the southeast. Captain Hunter looked at the direction of the wind and ship, and disappeared below. He had no intention of being around, checking up on what Mr. Sykes intended to do. And so Mr. Sykes ordered the squaresails set free and lowered to the deck and taken off. This was done in very smart fashion. One of the very great advantages of a schooner is that it can sail not only much closer to the wind than a square rigged ship, but it can sail so much faster. And now that we were going into a reach, which meant sailing partly on the wind, the sails were now useless. The booms on the mainsail and the foresail were hauled in close. The little ship heeled just a bit more and she ran noticeably faster. We sailed all day.

It was a beautiful late June day and, as we got farther out from civilization, we loaded our little cannon and fired once, without a ball. Later on, when we practiced in port, we would put a man ashore and fire into the sand dunes, and the man would watch where the ball went. Then he would dig it out and recover it, for a ball was too precious to be lost. When that little gun fired for the first time, its boom clattered up and down and back and forth across the sound, like so many shots in retaliation. We were so very proud of our little brass ten-pounder. We aimed at the gulls and fired all our muskets in practice, and I must say with all due modesty, that on two occasions, using the captain's long Lancaster County rifle, I knocked over two gulls riding in the water at about one hundred yards.

As darkness approached, we sailed into a bay on the Long Island shore which was about a quarter of a mile wide. It had a little curl forming a cove. So we sailed in and headed up into this curl. I realized again what a fine handling ship a schooner really is and how great an improvement it was over ships of any other size and rig. I saw this demonstrated time and again in the future in combat against brigs, barks, brigantines and barkintines, and when we were taking prizes. We dropped anchor, secured in Bristol fashion, and went to bed.

We sailed all the next day, the next night, the next day, and the next night. At times we could see the shoreline, first on one side and then another. But now the shoreline was disappearing entirely and the seas were long and rolling with white caps. The little ship was pitching along in an easterly direction, hard on the wind. We were taking long tacks and, after hours and hours of sailing, we would see a shoreline ahead. I was told that this was the Connecticut shore. Then we would go about and head on out to sea. After more hours of sailing, we could see a shoreline on the starboard side. We were now approaching the tip of Long Island.

My stomach was beginning to feel a little sick and I guess I was beginning to look a little strange, for the captain told me to stay on deck, and when I did not have duties to perform I was to sit amidship. There the boat would roll and rock about me and I would perceive the least motion. But as the time went on and the seas became steeper, I became ill. After visiting the rail a number of times, I lay prostrate on the deck. My stomach was heaving, but there was nothing to come up and I now had a violent headache.

I lay there unable to rise and presently the captain tapped me on the back. I looked up, feeling more dead than alive, but there was again that affectionate, sympathetic smile. He held a beaker in his hand and told me to drink without stopping. I later learned it was whiskey and laudinum. Soon after taking it, I threw part of it up, without being able to reach the rail. I wanted to wash down the deck, but a sailor stepped forward and threw a bucket of sea water on the deck and washed it down for me.

Presently I felt no more, and when I awakened, we were in a pleasant harbour. The motion of the ship had stilled and there were two or three other boats there. I heard men talking and I arose slowly, a little weak and a little dizzy. Richard helped me to the galley, where I had tea and food. I soon felt much better. No matter how many times I went to sea, if the motion was just right I would experience the same terrible condition. It never lasted but it frequently happened after leaving quiet water.

I looked out and there were windmills. I had never seen windmills before. Here were great turning windmills, as I had heard sailors from other parts of the world tell about while we were tied up in New York. I soon learned we were in Nantucket, and since I knew not where Nantucket was located, I searched out a chart and wondered what we were doing way over here. I thought we were going around the tip of Long Island and on out to sea. I soon learned the truth; the men were beginning to transfer the powder to other boats. I heard, they would land on the south shore of the cape, and they were going to tote it across to Boston, where it was to be used in the seige of Boston.

I saw our captain sign a paper, and I understood later that we retained ten kegs of powder for our own use. We were told when we went to Sagg Harbour that we would be entirely in friendly hands. A British lesser ship of the line had recently been captured by a group of intrepid men, so there we would receive additional cannon and arms. When I consulted the chart more closely, I realized that this little island of Nantucket, so far from shore and such a safe little haven, would soon be left behind and again we would go out to sea. When our captain found that I was so interested in windmills, he told me to go ashore, but only to inspect one windmill and come directly back because we might have to cast off in a hurry.

I went ashore and was delighted to see how the windmills were constructed. The little building was mounted on a swivel base, and a great wheel on the ground supported a long boom attached to the mill, so that two men could roll the great wheel and turn the little windmill house into the wind. This mill was used to grind corn and wheat. It could be turned into the wind or on the wind, depending upon the miller's desire for speed. I was fascinated by this little contraption and wondered if the windmills in Holland were built so they could be swiveled around and faced into the wind. Pictures I had seen failed to show this long boom arm, and the wheel at the end of the boom. According to the captain's instructions, I returned to the beach, stopping only long enough in the store on the edge of the beach to buy some sweets.

When the captain saw the promptness of my return, he smiled. He was well pleased.

After another good meal, I felt as strong as ever. The captain remarked that what I had felt would probably never occur again, but he was wrong. He said it had been good for me, most particularly for my liver, because it had "washed and cleansed me out." The following morning, after a good breakfast, we set sail on a westerly wind. Sailing on the quarter, with all sails set in only a slightly choppy sea, we were now on our way to Sagg Harbour.

It was another beautiful day with an azure sky. Scarcely a cloud interrupted the blueness, and the few that did were lovely white cotton balls, lazily hanging there, scarcely in motion. The sea was a painter's emerald green, the two colors harmonized well as they raced out to the horizon.

We sailed onward throughout the day, and late in the afternoon entered the bay to Sagg Harbour. Now I saw Indians, more than I had ever seen before. There were many Indians fishing along the beach, in canoes and in bateaus, gathering small fish with nets and seines, and spearing them. After we tied at the dock we saw as many Indians as white people there.

Lo and behold, lying very close to us was the British prize which had recently been captured. She was a first class ship of the line of fifty-two guns, and how any men could ever accomplish such a daring deed was more than I could then understand.

The captain told me to take a look about the town, but not to linger or tarry, and if I heard the firing of a gun, I was to come back as rapidly as I did that day in New York when I brought news from the town crier and leaped upon the deck. He smiled again as he said this. Now I was once again a sailor in a strange port, and I went forth to new adventures.

Sagg Harbour was made up of two general types of houses, the larger houses constructed of wood and owned by the sea captains, and the smaller homes owned by fishermen and tradespeople. They were strikingly similar to the smaller homes in our part of New Jersey, consisting of a long sloped roof with a lean-to in back and a front sharply-sloped roof, so that the effect was of an old-fashioned salt box. The more pretentious houses frequently had a widow's or captain's walk between the two chimneys on the roof top, allowing the wife to watch with a spyglass for the arrival of her husband's ship, or the captain to strut in his leisure and admire his ship in the harbor, or merely to survey the beautiful surrounding tidewater country and dream.

The houses weren't as pretentious as those of Nantucket, which were constructed of brick imported from England. Here, as there, the larger houses had beautiful central halls and centered doorways with two large windows on either side of the doors. The stoop or portico contained intricate hand-carvings of a pleasing design. My interest in architecture, even at this early age, was so profound that I was entranced by the beauty of the broken and full arched

*Salt Box House*

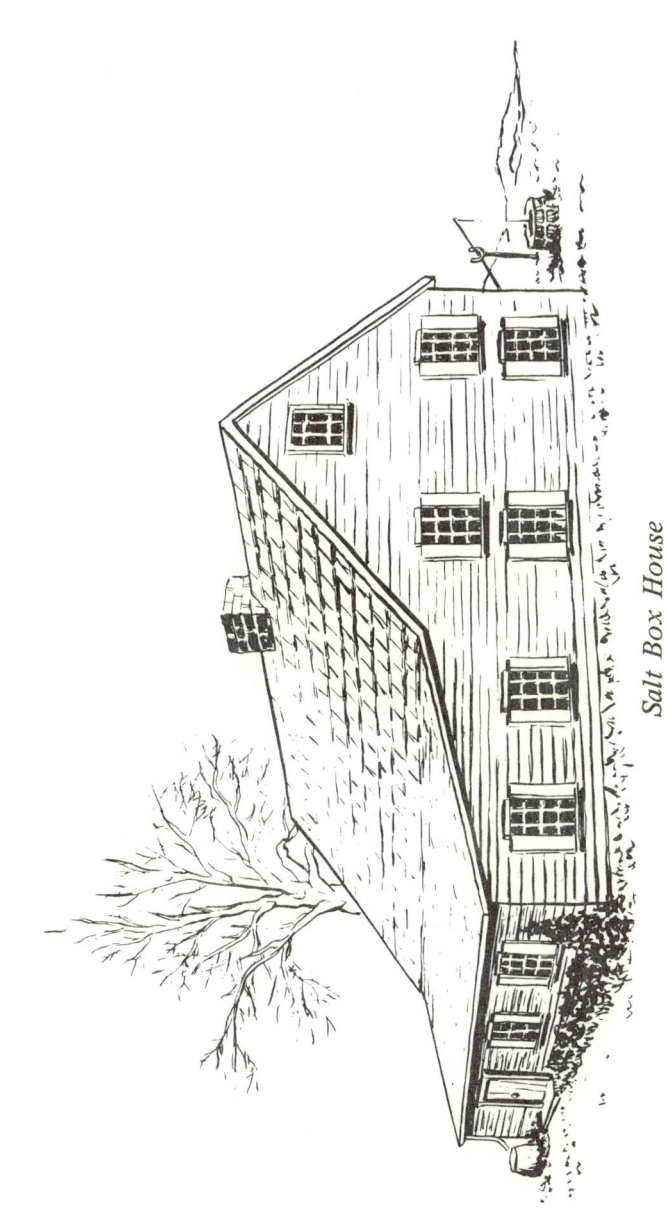

door frames. I later learned that most of these doorways had been constructed by two figurehead builders from Rhode Island by the names of Goddard and MacIntire.

In Sagg Harbour, many of these homes still carried the heavy paneled Indian blinds with the heavy hardware and the slits in the blinds to insert a musket. Even at this late date, there were occasional uprisings of the tribes.

There was one general store in the town which sold everything, as far as I could see. And as I walked into it, I was intrigued by the variety of its merchandise. There was food, clothing, equipment, powder, household things, liquor and beads for Indian wampum. Women's drawers hung next to boots, corsets were displayed next to lanterns, and I cast an eye on each.

There were many ships in the harbor, but there was no activity aboard; many looked as though they had been in port since before the embargo. They badly needed paint and repair. The people I saw on the village streets were gaunt, lean and serious looking, worried, cold, and unfriendly. Of course, these were trying times and it was very difficult for most people to make up their minds—their future was at stake.

I wandered back to our little ship and sat quietly on deck. About this time two men came aboard and asked for the captain, who immediately came up. The first man to speak was a tall, heavyset individual, who was apparently impressed with his own self-importance. He wanted to sign aboard. But Captain Hunter told the man that he wasn't suited for our particular job, so he disappeared over the side. The second man was small, not more than five feet six inches in height, but with an infectious smile and a ruddy complexion. His father had been a sea captain. And since he had sailed a great deal with his father, he knew these waters intimately. He also knew the waters of the Chesapeake Bay. He spoke modestly, confidently and with a certain amount of pride and assurance, but with not a word of conceit. I knew as the captain looked at him that he was already a member of the crew, and I was glad. "What is your name?" the captain asked softly.

"Louis R. Pearsall," he replied. He took out his papers, which were quite in order. He too was a mate, and a very qualified one at that. As the captain looked at them, he smiled and said, "We'll have all mates on this ship and no sailors."

But Mr. Pearsall quickly replied, "When I sign on, Captain, I sign on to fight. I'm willing to do anything, even holystone the decks."

"I know you're that kind of a man, Mr. Pearsall, and we all feel the same way. I know we'll be very happy to have you, and I hope you'll be very happy with us. Boy, show Mr. Pearsall to his bunk."

"Aye, aye, sir!"

I could see that the captain was very anxious to be on our way. I heard him discuss it with Mr. Sykes and Mr. Pearsall. Undoubtedly there would be hell to pay as soon as the British heard that the ship of the line had been captured. They would soon be in Sagg Harbour to probably burn it; therefore, it would be well to get out while we still could.

This was a characteristic of our captain. He was always most restless when he was in port, and calmest when he was at sea, particularly in action. The more difficult the action, the calmer he became.

Mr. Pearsall was the same kind of man. He rarely volunteered opinions and then only occasionally during a discussion, but when asked for one, as with Mr. Sykes, it always came without a moment's hesitation, and it was always right. I have seen him more than once when the going was tough, standing by the wheel on the poop deck, or leaning against the mast or the boom, smoking a twist of rolled tobacco.

We might be passing through dangerous inlets in heavy weather, but it made no difference to him. Once we were outside rounding the hook (Sandy Hook, New Jersey) after dark, with high crashing seas and an almost terrifying northwest wind. If he was concerned he never showed it; in action he was perfectly calm. At times the captain called him a "Long Island hard shell crab" or a "Chesapeake Bay shell-back," but always in the fondest terms. He was the kind of man who would give you his last dollar, but he had a dry kind of sarcasm which he let loose once or twice against the British. He was devoted to the ship and to us, and we were all devoted to him.

For supper, we had a fine mess of shedder crabs, homemade corn bread, fresh garden peas, Long Island potatoes, berry pie and coffee. Two men went on watch, one at the bow over the fo'c's'l, and one on the stern at the poop deck, the watch to be changed at midnight. The rest of us turned in and soon went to bed for we wanted to get an early start in the morning.

When I came on deck in the morning, I found the captain restlessly pacing the deck, anxious to get to sea. He would stop pacing from time to time, look in the direction of the inlet, and scan the horizon with his glass. I respectfully asked whether I could do anything for him, but he kindly said, "No, we'll be delayed almost another day. We should get out by dark. We have provisions to put aboard, something we all forgot about in our haste to get away. The fresh water casks and provisions will come early this morning, so this will give you another day ashore. Take advantage of it and enjoy yourself, but don't go out of gunshot range, for we may need you back here very quickly. There are many things for you to see, my boy. There are windmills and some houses built as early as 1650. Study carefully the architecture and make some sketches, for they'll stand you in good stead in later years. You won't always be a sailor. If you can get inside any of the houses, make a study of the staircases and the height of their risers and treads. By all means, see the windmills. Oh, yes, and study the hardware, for this section has beautiful, black iron hardware, made of high carbon material which doesn't rust even in the salt air. This hardware is made by the finest shipbuilders and men who make whaling tools. Now get your breakfast and be on your way."

*Barry University Library*
*Miami, FL 33161*

So I went ashore again at Sagg Harbour, an important and prosperous whaling port where sailors received $1.28 a day, and whale oil sold for twenty-eight dollars a barrel. The captains were able to build beautiful homes on the bluff overlooking this wide, beautiful harbor open to the east and northeast. Many of these were built a story high on granite blocks or bricks. A native told me that at least twice in one sailor's memory the storms here had come up the main street into the ground floor of the houses. As a result, most of the houses, particularly those of the prosperous, are built up a full story and backed against the side of the bluff. This way one can go out the back door and up the bluff from dry floor to dry land.

The houses were of two classes—the simple salt-box type, with its long sloping roof in back and its short front sloping roof, and the grand Greek Revival mansions with column fronts from ground to roof. The iron hardware was beautifully fashioned and seemed to be made by the same men who made the beautiful whaling harpoons and spears. Even the simple houses had Indian blinds. The more prosperous houses of the sea captains were after the fashion of Connecticut and Rhode Island, and most particularly of New London. These were generally frame houses with a captain's or widow's walk, ornate panel shutters or Indian blinds with iron hardware, and often containing cut-in seahorse or dolphin designs.

There was great activity in the streets. The whaling ships were getting ready to go to sea, having been bottled up by the proclamation of the King. But now, having heard that the ships in New London, Nantucket and Martha's Vineyard were going, the Sagg Harbour men intended to sail again out of sheer defiance. It was whispered and rumored that just as soon as Congress could agree on something, and pass an order or an edict recognizing privateering, they would all be privateers.

As I looked down from the hill toward our ship, the British frigate was rapidly being dismantled and everything of usefulness, down to the last gun, was being divided as spoils and passed out to various ships. Presently I saw a great sight ahead—a windmill turning! The wind was rather brisk at this season of the year and I ran up the street like a madman, for I knew not when the volley of the musket might sound and I would have to return to the ship. I soon came upon this great windmill. The miller was standing in the doorway, and several Indians were standing about with bags in hand. I later learned that they were waiting for the sweepings from the corn, wheat and rye flour.

"Boy, come in," said the miller. "You've never seen one of these before, have you?"

"No, sir."

"Be careful of the cogs and gears. What ever you do, don't get near them. A man over Easthampton way was killed last year in the most horrible manner. His screeches could be heard for half a mile as he wound slowly between the cogs and gears." I felt weak all over—this should have been enough to frighten me back to the ship. I saw the chaff separated from the corn or wheat. Then the chaff ran out the end and into another bin. This was what the Indians were waiting for. Of course, the chaff contained a considerable amount of food; much of the material had failed to grind completely. (Under present day knowledge, the Indians were getting some of the best parts.)

The miller wanted me to stay. He told me I was a bright boy, that he would like to make a miller out of me and teach me to build mills. He asked me where I came from. When I told him between Woodbridge and Perth Amboy, he said, "Boy, you don't have mills down there, do you?"

"No, sir," I said.

"But you have lots of air," and he laughed.

"Yes, sir."

"Then why wouldn't that be a fine place for you to go back to, after you learn the business, and make mills?"

I told him that when the war was over I might come back. And so, rather sorry to leave, I strolled down the main street, my hands in my pockets, and back toward our little ship. What a little ship it seemed as it stood alongside the great British man-of-war.

I approached the customs house at the foot of the main street facing the beautiful harbor. This building was constructed of brick and granite brought over from Connecticut.

As I stood on the corner about to say farewell to the town, perhaps for the last time, I met a man who seemed to be a farmer in town for the day, but it soon turned out that he was an old friend and distant relative of Mr. Pearsall. I believe his name was Will Freedell, and he told me the story of how our intrepid boys in the six whale boats had captured this mighty man-of-war.

It seems that the British General Erskine, before his invasion of this end of Long Island, sent a warship down to Gardner's Island and placed a detail ashore. The idea was to watch for whale boat men who might be carrying on local privateering. The British continued to put details ashore at other islands. The whale boat men learned that the officers went ashore night after night and left the ship illy manned, with only a young deck officer and a few men in charge.

The following morning these men put out from near the New London shore with six whale boats and crews and sailed across the sound. Arriving toward night, they came alongside the warship, hoisted the British flag, and when the young officer came on deck, the leader reprimanded him for keeping such an ill ship. The officer thought he was a customs inspector and, defending the condition of his ship, invited the captain aboard. The captain and the militiamen swarmed aboard and quickly captured the ship. They then up-anchored and sailed her into Sagg Harbour. When they arrived, there was the dilemma. Sagg Harbour was a small town with very few inhabitants. The people had already received reprisals for what little aid they had given their fellow colonists; the British had slain some of their men on the beaches, and hung some of them in front of the Customs House. Thus the Connecticut men decided that it would be safer for them to take the blame since they were difficult to reach, even though Sagg Harbour and Easthampton men had taken an important part in the raid. The town feared, as my good captain had stated earlier, that the British would soon arrive in their whale boats. Then there would be hell to pay. So our whale boat men decided to sail her out in the night, after having stripped her and divided her armament among the whalers and other ships, and then scuttle her by fire. I thanked Mr. Freedell and hurried on to my ship.

It was late in the afternoon when I arrived back. Although I had never ventured more than a quarter of a mile, the captain was glad to see me. He was greatly excited and said that come evening they were going to sail out the man-of-war and set fire to her. We would sail with her, with the tide, and be on our way to sea. The sun was going down and the evening was cold; it was now late October. Presently large bands of men appeared and a string of whale boats was attached to this great ship. As the sun sank beyond the horizon and darkness came out of the east, they set sail, the string of whale boats towing the great ship. We set sail with them.

It was a great satisfaction for me to see the words of our captain so admirably confirmed once again. In a short time we had outsailed her by a great distance. Within a space of half an hour we were at least as far ahead of her as she was from the shore. We were sailing right into the open sea. It was calm October weather with steady westerly winds, but cold. Of course, she was not sailing to the best of her advantage, for she was carrying reduced canvas. But on the other hand, all the men who were sailing her were real sailors. They were sailing men from Sagg Harbour, Stonington, New London, and other smaller towns of Mystic and Lime along the Connecticut shore. They were men who had been to sea many times and aboard whalers for many years, and they showed the hardship in their faces and their brawn in the strength of their muscles.

We were approaching the open sea now and off to the south we could just see Montauk Indian Point, the high long point of the tip of Long Island. The other islands were dropping away fast and the great British ship was falling rapidly behind. Our captain looked strained and worried and all the men seemed to sense it. He constantly scanned the horizon and we learned, as time went on, that this meant he had a premonition of things to come.

"Mr. Pearsall, can we sail close under the lee of that point or must we stand off?" asked Captain Hunter.

"You can sail right along the beach, Captain. Even at low water with our draft, we're just as safe off the beach as a mile off."

"Thank you, Mr. Pearsall," said the captain.

"Thar she goes, Captain," said Mr. Sykes.

And as we all turned to look back, a shudder went through my body. It started in the top of my head under my cap, swept downward through my spine and out my arms, down my back, across my stomach, down my legs and to the soles of my feet. My teeth chattered and I felt weak. I held onto the rail. We all looked sad and startled. The flames were reaching up into the rigging and the vast columns of smoke and tongues of fire could be seen in the evening light. The burning continued and reached a great climax, like the onset of a storm or the crescendo of a church organ. Then the color and glow began to fade in the early evening darkness. A thousand embers sprayed from the burning ship; some went out as they passed through the air and some as they struck the water. We saw the great fiery masts topple over, one after another. Then the fire went down, but it flared up once or twice. We all stood in awe, scarcely able to tend to our ship as we grouped together on the stern. Finally the glow disappeared, the fire died out, and the night was still. We were sailing along in the darkness now and we could see the lights in one or two farmhouses, for we were close to the shore.

The first one to speak was Captain Hunter. "It seems a shame that a ship like that, which could do us all so much good, had to be scuttled, yet there was nothing else that could be done. The Continental Congress hasn't yet made up its mind as to whether we'll stay with England or divorce ourselves from the mother country. It hasn't made up its mind yet whether it will take us in as a part of the American navy or whether we must refrain or operate as pirates. To prevent this ship, in a short time, from being returned to His Majesty's service, it was necessary to strip and bury her. I've expected all day that the British will shortly come to Sagg Harbour and punish innocent people. If they do, I for one, will retaliate vigorously the moment we go into service.[3] Mr. Pearsall, do you think we're far enough off the point?"

"Yes, Captain. We're just about right."

"I should say if we hold this course until that farm house light disappears, we can round the point and head on out to sea."

"Where to, Captain?" asked John Hunter.

"Well, let's decide that right here, while we're all together. Call up Richard. He has as much right to be a part of this discussion as anyone else." I bolted down from the poop deck and returned promptly with him.

"Gentlemen, I hope you will agree with me in my selection of our next port. The nights are becoming colder. Before long there will be much ice and we can do no one any good up here. We are outcasts from our own home. Certainly by this time, the colonial governor of New Jersey has discovered that we are doing more than carrying a load of bricks from Peekskill to New York. Certainly the Tory spies around New York know it also. I daresay that the few Tory spies located around old Sagg Harbour have gone by horse and sail to tell the King's men all about us. Therefore, there is only one port left for us, and I'm afraid that for the rest of the war it will be our home. If our families wish to see us, this is the port to which they will have to come."

Everyone was leaning forward. What port could it be? We were looking at each other now. It couldn't be near New York. Captain Hunter was having a good time with us, but finally he spoke. "Little Egg Harbour, New Jersey.'

The men who had sailed with the captain before promptly nodded their heads in agreement and I found myself nodding too, as though I were a person of some

*39*

importance. Poor Richard just smiled, happy because everyone agreed.

The captain scratched his head, shifted his hat, and pulled his coat a little closer about his neck, and so did we all, for it was really cold now. "You men took the wind out of my sails. I didn't expect such quick agreement, but apparently you see it as clearly as I do, but for Mr. Pearsall, Richard, and the boy, I would like to explain my position.

"Little Egg Harbour is a great port of call. From there, American ships sail not only coastwise, but in foreign trade. It's a great fitting-out center so there's ample timber and bog iron close by. We will be in friendly hands and, except for the Pine Barons, the Pine Robbers and the Beach Pirates, all of whom you will hear about in due time, we couldn't be in a more suitable position, both offensively and defensively. We will be almost an equal distance between the Delaware and New York inlet. No great ships could ever follow us into the bay, for it's too shoal. There are hundreds of miles of inland waters defensible in great forests, and hiding places in the great marshes and the tall reeds. A schooner, with its crossarms lowered to the deck, can stand among the trees and can rarely be seen, even with a spyglass. I was once looking for a captain friend of mine, and I hunted for hours in the middle of the day. The spars and his ship were so well hidden I would never have found him if a friendly Indian hadn't come along and directed me.

"Mr. Pearsall, would you take your trick at the wheel, and John, you stay on deck with Mr. Pearsall. Go forward and watch over the bow."

"Yes, sir."

"Aye, aye, sir."

"Whether we are asleep or awake, if anything at all unusual occurs, call us at once. The rest of you men had better turn in. But first, let's go down by the fire, get warm, and have something to eat."

The main cabin of our little ship had a comfortable fireplace and a gorgeous mantel with hand-carvings of fans and shells across the frontpiece. The moldings were intricate and detailed, just enough in size and amount to set off the mantel. The fluting and the reeding up the side supports looked like the beautiful columns of a Grecian temple. It was painted white and, against the rich salmon red brick set in the white mortar, it stood out exquisitely. It was the only home we had, and how we delighted to get into the captain's cabin.

Our captain has been influenced by his trips to Newport, by the Goddard School of Design, by Townsend and the rest of the house and ship carpenters. He had also been influenced by Nathaniel Dominy, a well known designer of windmills and a silversmith down at South and East Hampton, Long Island. He was also a furniture and cabinet maker. He made as fine doorways as Goddard and Townsend and worked on ship interiors, the great whalers and the coastwise traders before the embargo. Our captain knew him, for he had been the chief cabinet maker in New Jersey.

The main cabin was panelled beyond the fireplace with hand-rubbed walnut. The sloping sides of this fine ship formed the two opposite walls of the cabin and contained just the right curvature for us to lean back and rest. (Now that I was seventeen, I, too, had my long church warden clay pipe.) All the comforts of home had been built into this ship. The table upon which the charts could be spread was a fine eighteenth century Chippendale with flaring legs. The tables on either side of the fireplace were of the late Queen Anne or Chippendale school and they were bolted to the floor, as was all the other furniture. Upon them, held firmly by little brackets, were our whale oil lamps, which gave the cabin ample illumination.

After having smelled a spermaceti candle burning, the captain would have no part of them. He said, "I'd rather go back to farming . . . and never sail on a ship again than to burn a spermaceti candle. It smells like herring."

Frequently when we were in tight spots, or had just gotten out of one, and were tired and discouraged, or when we were celebrating a victory, our captain would bring forth some bayberry candles and, instead of eating in the galley or forward in the crew's quarters, we would all eat in the main cabin.

Richard would sit on the companionway stairs leading down from the poop deck. But although he was invited on many occasions, he wouldn't sit at the table. He always gave one excuse or another; he needed more room or the inlet wasn't wide enough.

All at once the captain spoke up and renewed the conversation about the great British frigate which had been set on fire. "You know, men, if I had known early enough that they were going to scuttle her, I would have asked for the furnishings in her captain's quarters. They were certainly beautiful. The captain had a magnificent mahogany four-poster bed built on a swivel so that as the ship rolled, it would remain on an even keel. It was an elegant Chippendale. And there was a lovely sofa in the chart room." The captain smiled.

"The design of this sofa was very charming. It had the flowing ends of Chippendale. There was also a fine chest on frame of the Sheraton or Chippendale school, with the most exquisite lead glass bottles I ever saw. There were twelve bottles with twelve of the most intricately handcut glass stoppers, all filled with liqueurs. The captain's desk was a beauty. It was also Chippendale, with a sloped top. It could have come right out of Boston; it was as much in design like our original old Winthrop desks as anything could possibly be. We made a lot of them in our cabinet shop, remember, boy?"

"Yes, sir," I said, for I remembered well.

"The drapes in that main saloon were quite something, and to think the entire ship went up in flame and smoke." He paused. "I noticed a shift in our course a little while ago, Mr. Sykes."

"I presume the men are changing course now for Little Egg."

"Boy, go on deck and tell the men to hold our course for

the southwest, and try to hold it on that course as much as possible."

"Yes, sir."

I delivered the message and returned. Orders were now given for the second watch and the other men were advised to turn in. There was a general lift to the ship, followed by a slow pleasant fall. I sat on the companionway stairs, with the wind whistling gently through the rigging and the billowing white sails, pulling for all they were worth. The last rays of day had long since faded and the stars were out.

The captain came to the companionway. "Boy," he said, "you'd better stand with the men on this first watch. You're seventeen now and your responsibilities will become greater all the time. I also suggest that during the day you practice with your long rifle, that reliable Lancaster County musket.[4] Practice shooting gulls—before long it may be your duty to sit or stand in the yardarms and pick our enemy away from their guns."

I drew my coat around me and went on deck, made my way aft to the wheel, and stood there with the men. They were talking of home and it made me desperately homesick. I took a deep breath and stood up like a man, I hoped, then looked off across the vast sea with stern face and thin drawn mouth, like the other men who were thinking of home.

I wondered how my mother and my sisters were. My mother hadn't been too well when I left. I thought about my sisters and brothers and thought how beautiful my sisters were. Then I thought of the girls in Sagg Harbour and how beautiful they were. I thought of one girl in particular who had smiled at me rather sheepishly. A funny feeling came over me and I remembered a lot of things my brothers had told me. I also remembered a great many things Captain Hunter had told me from time to time. I finally got my mind off this subject and looked at the stars. I watched the water rushing by under the rail, took a deep breath, and began to ask the men questions related to navigation and sailing by the stars, and they began to explain. The stars were so far away, they could be considered fixed points. Therefore, it was easy to take these points as parts of a triangle and measure distance. When the watch was changed, I went on to bed, thinking that some day I, too, might be a good sailor or a great captain and walk the deck of my own ship. I hoped that I might be as fine a man as Captain Hunter, Mr. Sykes, or Mr. Pearsall.

My mother had sent along two featherbeds, for she wanted me to be as comfortable as possible. I slept with one under me and one over me and, indeed, I was very comfortable. Scarcely had I hit my bed when, almost like the effect of laudinum, I slowly and happily fell off to sleep.

# 4

*I was awakened* after midnight, sometime after the second watch, by the cry, "All hands on deck!" As I jumped to the floor I was conscious of a great rolling and pitching of the ship, and the sound of water crashing on the outside of the hull. I pulled on my trousers and rushed on deck. The wind was high and had evidently shifted and was now coming out of the northeast; with it came a snow flurry. The wind was very cold. I was called to the bow at the foresail and there took part in tying down a reef. The reefs were soon secured and the outer jib was taken off. What little I could see in the darkness beyond our little ship was boiling white water. We were driving along at great speed but pitching and yawing. After we secured the outer jib and reefed the foresail, I went aft with the rest of the crew. I thought how terrible it would be to fall overboard while securing a jib. You would almost certainly go under the ship and not have a chance in the darkness.

Poor Richard was not only very sick, but very frightened, and as he looked out into the cold darkness he exclaimed, "The fishes wool make a fuss over me."

This became a byword with the crew. When we were passing through boiling inlets, through great crashing breakers or roaring white water, one crest upon the next, rolling down into the quiet troughs like the spread of oil on water, first one member of the crew and then the other would remark, "The fishes wool make a fuss over me." This became a pleasant addition to a sometimes monotonous life and I think it pleased Richard very much.

It was very cold, the wind was high, and the spray from the crashing waves against our little ship wet us through and through. I was very cold and, happily, we were ordered back to our bunks. I was so grateful that my mother had sent along those two fluffy featherbeds with a fine big feather bolster for a pillow. I pulled off my wet trousers and, in my nakedness, crawled between the goose feathers. I realized that with all this pitching and yawing, I was not a bit sick. Soon I was again lost in the happy slumber of youth.

At breakfast, the captain assured us that just as soon as we got to Little Egg Harbour it would be warm and beautiful, and the pine air would invigorate us all. That was another reason he wanted to make that port our home. In the quiet freshwater creeks and bays, the barnacles would rapidly fall off the hull, while we lay in quiet and warmth among the pines and waited for our orders as privateersmen.

The day broke bright and clear, and the wind was still northeast. There were a few snow clouds in the sky, but it was definitely warmer. We were feeling the effects of the Gulf Stream water, although we were only on the edge. Actually, we were probably about fifty miles from the stream, but the effect could still be felt. We crashed along, lifting and falling, rolling occasionally from side to side, but it was pleasant. She was a gallant ship and she took it all with no water over her stern. She did not dip down by the bow, although the seas were long, steep following ones and they bowled us along. Sometime during breakfast, the men on deck had set the foresquaresail and the topsail and had put out the outer jib. We were still carrying the reefs in the foresail and the mainsail; these additional sails not only increased our speed but steadied our ship.

Richard was still very sick and the captain talked to him very sympathetically. He told Richard that if he wished, he might stay in his bunk, but that he thought he would be better on deck, out in the fresh air, and to lie midship across the deck where the roll was least. He was given a dose of laudinum and covered over with a great blanket made from our own sheep, and in a short time poor Richard was sleeping soundly.

I don't remember who scurried up the breakfast that morning, but it was a good one. It didn't have the Richard touch, but it was still a good breakfast.

That morning we spotted a ship on the horizon. She seemed to be a large merchantman, and through the glass we saw she carried the royal ensign of the British Crown. We flew no flag and carried no pennant. She was most likely an armed merchantman sailing for New York or Boston. But we did not alter our course and in a short while we were each hull down on the horizon. We were all on deck now, sitting about smoking and enjoying the lovely day.

Evidently during the night the wind had been very high, for the seas were still very steep and crashing. I wanted to look at a chart to see the direction in which Little Egg Harbour Inlet lay, for I could conceive of nothing worse than going through a bad inlet with these following seas.

There was work to be done, so we arose, stretched, and the group broke up. Mr. Sykes remarked, "I think we might shake out the reefs, Captain. The wind is slackening off."

"You're quite right, Mr. Sykes. Go right ahead and do it now."

I looked over the side as I walked forward and noticed that the seas, although they were still rolling, were no longer crashing and the white caps had just about disappeared. We shook out the reefs and boxed the two mainsails on either side of our little ship, for we were riding full before the wind. We all took up our stations at the sails in order to keep them full and the log was thrown over the rail. The captain, Mr. Sykes and Mr. Pearsall took out their watches and counted the knots. Presently the log was pulled in and the watches compared, and as the day wore on the captain announced that we were making about 8½ knots (10 miles). It was a beautiful late October day. The sky was clear and the storm clouds had vanished. Having sailed all night, and now all day, we began to see land.

There were long sloping, scalloped sand dunes, but not a sign of life. Far behind the dunes we could see the multicolored fall changes in the trees. Here and there were great patches of evergreens, and we knew we were well down the Jersey coast. Flight after flight of geese were going south, and further inland nearer the shore, tremendous flights of ducks were going in the same direction. The men remarked that they would like to have some duck or goose and the captain, overhearing this, called down from the poop deck, "Wait until we get into Tuckerton Bay and in the fresh marshes of Little Egg. After they've been feeding on wild rice and have fresh water for two or three days, the odor and taste of fish will leave their bodies. In about a week we'll have the finest fresh duck and goose anyone could ask for." And so we did!

On more than one occasion, the crew was struck by the diversified and complete information which the captain possessed. As I have said before, he was almost always right.

"Captain, there's white water ahead," said Mr. Sykes. "I believe we're almost off Barnegat."

"Yes, Mr. Sykes. I agree."

This long stretch of beach must certainly be the stretch from the Hook to Barnegat. The men looked at their watches. (Someday I want to own a fine large watch made by one of the Philadelphia or New York watchmakers.) The sea was levelling off more and more all the time because the bottom was nearer the top, but the wind was holding. We were really "loping" along at a great clip. We went down for our midday meal. The captain had not yet come down, so Mr. Sykes said, "We've had it pretty easy so far. I suggest as soon as we get in, select a favorable anchorage

and tie up, we put this ship once more in Bristol fashion."
Mr. Pearsall replied, "I always did like to holystone a deck. Boy, did you ever holystone a deck?"
"No, sir."
"Well, you're going to learn."
They all laughed. I laughed too, but not later when I holystoned the deck.[5] Presently, standing in the doorway with a weak but kindly smile, was our old friend, Richard. Everyone spoke at once. "How do you feel, Richard?"
"I feel tolerable better. I'll get you men something to eat."
"No, you won't Richard. Sit down there on your favorite spot on the stair. Boy, get Richard a slug of rum."
"Yes, sir."
Although before that time I had never seen Richard take a drink, he did as instructed. In a very short time he felt much better and was busy with the midday meal.

I finished, returned to the deck, and realized how fast we were really moving. The crashing, ominous breakers of Barnegat were far behind and I realized that by the time we reached Little Egg, the sea would not be too alarming to enter the inlet. I offered to take a trick at the wheel and the helmsman was very pleased to have the relief. I took over and we continued sailing throughout the afternoon without seeing a vessel. We sailed along the beautiful pine-covered Long Beach Island and in the late afternoon uneventfully entered the inlet of Little Egg, in the face of a forest of tall-masted ships. The sight of this great port almost took my breath away.

We sailed up the harbor to the town dock in a creditable fashion, came about and made fast. We were the latest comer and so from the streets of the town we could see everyone running toward us in order to obtain news.

A boy was selling *The Pine's Courier* but I didn't buy one. My few coins were tightly sealed in my small purse and could not be wasted on newspapers.

Everything secured, the captain recommended that we each write a letter home at once. He instructed me to take them ashore to the inn, in order that they might be on the first stage to Trenton and then northward to our homes.

In a short while everyone reappeared on deck and I assembled the letters. The people were standing on the wharf, waiting for news. The captain graciously stood at the rail and spoke to them as though he were standing on a podium.

"We have come from Sagg Harbour. A great ship of the British line has been captured by Connecticut men who went across the sound in whale boats. After all usuable material was taken from it and supplied to the various ships of our enterprise, she was then taken out beyond Gardner's Island and burned."

The hurrahs were tremendous, supplemented by the raucous whistling of the boys. "I'm sorry I have no other news—except that we are here to await the orders of the Continental Congress and their wishes, and to sign on men and do our small part for the American Navy."

As the people looked at the tininess of the ship, they hurrahed, whistled again, and clapped and lifted their hats. We all stood by the rail, Richard in the background, returning the salutes with a lifting of hats and a discreet bowing of the heads and bodies.

As the captain picked up the newspaper, he exclaimed, "Listen to this! 'On the ninth of August the *Falcon* was seen in chase of two schooners bound to Salem. One of these was taken. A fair wind wafted the other into Gloucester Harbor. Lindzee, the Loyalist captain of the *Falcon*, followed with his prize and, after anchoring, sent his lieutenant with 36 men in a whale boat and two barges to bring under his bow the schooner that had escaped. As the bargemen, armed with muskets and swivels, boarded her at her cabin windows, men fired on them from the shore, killing three and wounding the lieutenant in the thigh. Upon this, Lindzee sent his prize and a cutter to cannonade the town. The broadside which followed did little injury. The Gloucester men kept up the fight for hours and, with a loss of but two, they took both schooners, the cutter, the barges, and every man in them. Lindzee lost 35 men, or half his crew, and the next day he sailed off carrying away no spoils except the skiff in which his wounded lieutenant was brought away.' Here is an example, men, of great discretion, planning, courage and fortitude, and we can do the same with the elements of surprise and planning. I've said it right along." He was evidently well pleased by this item in the paper, for it strengthened his fondest expectations of what we might be able to do.

It was common conversation about the town that Gage, in order to terrify the Americans and cheer his own soldiers, was telling of the arrival of thousands of Russian, Hessian and Hanovarian troops. Bottled up in Boston, he vented his ill-humor on his prisoners, throwing officers of high rank indiscriminately into felons' jail, there to languish with their wounds and even undergo amputations.

We also learned of the action taken by the Rhode Island Assembly. In June it had directed its own Committee of Safety to charter and outfit two armed vessels to protect the trade of the colony. The legislature of Connecticut ordered the equipment of two armed vessels for the defense of its seacoast, and the same month the Committees of Safety of South Carolina and Georgia were to "send out cruisers and watch for ships expected with gunpowder." Early in August General Washington proposed that Rhode Island should attempt the hazardous project of seizing the public magazine at New Providence (Bermuda). "We are in a situation which requires us to run all risks," he said.

Before it could be carried out, George Ord and Robert Morris, in a sloop dispatched from Philadelphia, and under the pretense of a trading voyage to New Providence, had taken the magazine by surprise. Then, in conjunction with a schooner from South Carolina, they had carried off more than one hundred barrels of powder. On the twenty-sixth, Rhode Island instructed its delegates in Congress to propose a Continental navy. In September, General Washington had instructed Broughton of Marblehead, an army captain, to take command of the detachment of their army Colonials (our first marines) and, in a schooner equipped at Continental expense, to intercept all vessels "laden" with supplies for the British army. Other vessels were employed under the Congress with good success. It was evident that our good captain was highly pleased with these newspaper reports because it showed that the birth of privateering was at hand.

It was only a matter of time now before we would be doing likewise. A courier rode in late one afternoon. The town bell sounded and we all rushed to the square. Here we learned that "Gage had returned to England and the new command had been given to Howe. The campaign was to be transferred to New York, but because of the lack of supplies and the unseasonable weather, Howe decided to remain in Boston for the winter. The British, burning with hate after the defeat of Lindzee, went up to Portland, began a cannonading on the sixteenth of October, and destroyed the town and the ships in the harbor.' This item in the local newspaper caused our captain to burn with rage. He paced the deck, slapping the paper against his side, and called for retaliation. He continued reading aloud: "The cannonading which started in the morning was kept up until dark. St. Paul's Church, the public buildings, and about 130 dwelling houses, about three-quarters of the town, were burned down. The remaining were completely shattered by shell and ball. With the beginning of the winter, the inhabitants were turned out of their homes and reduced to poverty and misery."

The paper also said that General Washington called these savage cruelties 'The exertion of despotic barbarity." And Greene said, "Death and destruction mark the paths of the enemy."

Sullivan was sent to fortify Portsmouth. Trumbull of Connecticut took over the defense of New London and patriots now held sway in Philadelphia at the Continental Congress.

On the third of October, one of the delegates from Rhode Island laid before the Congress his instructions to use their influence "to build and equip an American fleet."

*Little Egg. From the dunes across the bay.*

This was the origin of our navy. This proposal met with great opposition, but John Adams debated it readily and pursued it unremittingly, though "for a long time against wind and tide."

On the fifth, Washington was authorized to employ two armed vessels to intercept a British store ship bound for Quebec. And on the thirteenth, the Continental Congress voted for two armed vessels of 10 to 14 guns; then seventeen days later, two others of 36 guns.

But much time would pass before their equipment was complete. As yet, no court had the power to condemn vessels taken from the enemy, nor was war waged on the high seas, reprisals authorized, or our ports open to foreign nations.

Under the general's powers of command, Washington had hired vessels and men. They were already capturing British vessels and he now wished to appoint courts for the condemnation of these prizes.

This was the state of affairs at Little Egg the first part of November, 1775. Since Little Egg was such an important seaport and on a direct road from Trenton and Philadelphia, couriers brought news in almost daily, and each succeeding day the news was more and more startling.

November was passing. The weather was becoming cold even down here, but we were very comfortable. There was plenty of wood for the fireplace, plenty of food and fresh game, and we ate well. We kept our boat in top shape, and when the weather was particularly mild, we painted, tarred, and pitched her. She was as dry below the floor as she was above and never required any pumping or bailing.

I went forth every day throughout the town and along the waterfront, and got a view of the ships and talked to the sailors. Occasionally a new ship would come in. Still, idleness is a companion to lonesomeness and homesickness. There just wasn't enough to do, and so my homesickness returned.

None of us had heard from home and I imagine the other men were just as homesick and anxious as I. Just outside the town there were blacksmiths, shipbuilders, and a ropewalk. I had never seen rope made and it was indeed a fascinating enterprise. I watched the gunsmiths bore and ream the barrels and file the locks. Outside of town were the charcoal burners, the native people who made charcoal, one of the necessary products for the making of gunpowder. On the edge of town were the bog-iron furnaces and I spent many hours watching the processing. To think we could get iron from the roasting of bog by throwing oyster and clam shells into the fire was almost beyond my powers of comprehension. There were also the great shipyards anticipating the advent of an American navy.

There was a factory for processing sassafras, which was exported to Holland and made into a drink called sloop (now root beer). Great piles larger than haystacks were stored behind the factory. The streets of the town were of a clay kind of gravel which packed and made a very hard and durable road, with no rutting in bad weather. The houses were simple and I recall only one elaborate manor or mansion type of house. The sides of all the houses were clapboard or shingle. The houses were neatly painted and surrounded by picket fences. Altogether it was a plain, but very busy, bustling town. As the days wore on, I was very happy that our captain had selected this port as home, for although the sun was going further south every day, it was still quite warm, particularly in the middle of the day.

On the fifteenth of December we received glad tidings. A number of letters came in on the same coach from the families of our men. They all said about the same thing. Our families were leaving at once in a large frontier wagon, the property of my Aunt Kate (Hunter), and for us not to worry because they were being accompanied by two men, former members of the British army who had deserted and who were now courting daughters of members of the crew. One was a Hessian, the other an Englishman. In previous correspondence, Captain Hunter had instructed his wife that if they came down at any time, they were to follow the route which he had outlined. This route would take them along the way least traveled by the Pine Robbers. They were to bring ample young, strong and lively horses so that they could leave the stage stops with the stage and the couriers and stay with them. They were not to proceed alone and never any distance after dark.

Aunt Kate owned a large frontier wagon which had been built in the carriage shop of the Dunhams in Woodbridge. Aunt Kate, of a roving disposition, had decided to pull up stakes and go to the territory west of the Alleghenies which was being opened up and which George Washington had surveyed as a young man. Some of it would now become public grants. With the sudden turn of events, she had postponed her trip, had gotten the women together and decided that this was the wagon in which they should make the trip to Little Egg. The other families agreed.

And so, on the twelfth of December they all departed from Woodbridge: the Sykes family from Cranesford, the Hunter family from Perth Amboy, the Springers from Rahway, Richard's wife, Martha, sixteen ladies in all, accompanied by two former British soldiers. Aunt Kate at the reins, driving six horses, sat on the box. They crossed the sail ferry above Amboy to the little hamlet on the other side and proceeded on to Middletown Point. From there their route took them to Freehold, which was then called Monmouth Court House. Starting before daybreak they reached Freehold at nightfall. They put up there at Augie Desener's inn, tired but enthusiastic.

At daybreak they were off again on a good road and they now rolled through farming country on an almost straight road to New Egypt, where they arrived early the second day. There they made arrangements to proceed with the coach, the couriers, the Liberty Boys and a small detachment of mounted militia which was going through to Egg Harbour. This was the pine forest, the country of the Pine Barons and Robbers. The militia was to be stationed there as a protection to this important post. It was evident that the strategic location of this town was such that after the burning of New England towns, Egg Harbour must have greater protection. So the following morning the caravan started out from New Egypt at a leisurely pace across the Pine Barrens. The road was sandy and in places so low that logs had been laid crossways forming a corduroy. In spite of this, the road was very bad in spots because it received a great amount of traffic, and although it was improved from time to time because it was a necessary road for the many manufacturers of bog-iron, the cutting of timber, the gathering of sassafras, the collection of pine for turpentine and pitch, and the collection of wood for the charcoal burners, it was still not a good road.

Each day we anxiously scanned this road. A man was kept posted on the edge of town constantly during the daylight hours. Late in the afternoon, just about dark, on the afternoon of the fifteenth day of December, 1775, the caravan rolled into town. Far out in front came the dust-covered hard riding couriers and Liberty Boys on sweating horses. They came in, neck and neck. A short distance up the road came the post coach and right behind it was the big frontier wagon and the militia, the Jersey Blues. They raced along the last stretch, down the main street of town, the wagon rocking, swaying and bouncing along in an alarming manner; the girls and women hanging out the back yelling and crying with delight, many with tears in their eyes. Aunt Kate was sitting up on the box alongside the one driver, with a Committee of Safety musket[6] across her lap. Her face wore a great sense of pride and triumph as the wagon came to a sudden stop. The tail gate swung down and the girls leaped to the ground. Aunt Kate hoisted her skirts and jumped down from the box. The boys and men whistled, for although her hair contained streaks of gray, her face was as clear and unmarked by wrinkles as a maiden and her legs were just about perfect.

There was a great deal of hugging and caressing and the townspeople gathered around. They were happy in their holiday spirit and everyone offered to put them up, but the captain thanked them one and all and replied that he had made reservations for all at the inn. The hugging and the kissing went round and round, and although many of us had never met the complete party, we found we were hugging and kissing one another, then asking names afterward.

This was to be a long remembered Christmas. The one thing that the ladies and the two soldiers seemed most interested in was the difference in temperature. They had left snow and sleet, and here they were in a spring day, for this was the characteristic temperature of this beautiful little section, close by the sea and nestled in the pines.

I can't begin to tell you the wonderful Christmas we had. We all had our families, except for Mr. Pearsall, but the ladies all went out of their way to make him happy and comfortable. He enjoyed himself just as much as we did, and the holiday went by too rapidly.

New Year's Day, January, 1776, was a happy one, for the tri-colored American banner was unfurled over the new Continental army in Boston. It was not yet spangled with stars but showed thirteen stripes of alternate red and white in the field and the united red and white crosses of Saint George and Saint Andrew on a blue background in the corner. At that moment the army consisted of but 9,600 men, and on that day free Negroes stood in the ranks beside the white men. Three days later this happy event was to be marred by the news brought from Norfolk by courier. We assembled on the dock.

"New Year's Day, 1776," he began, "was the saddest day that ever broke on the women and children of Norfolk, Virginia. The British commander of a squadron warned that he would attack the town. Still there was no place for the women and children to go. The *Kingfisher* was stationed at the upper end of Norfolk. A little below was the *Otter*; farther below was the *Liverpool*; anchored at the middle of town was the *Dunmore*. The Royal Governor of Virginia was aboard the latter, having fled from the Assembly at Williamsburg in fear of the patriots. The rest of the fleet was moored in the harbor. Between three and four in the afternoon the *Liverpool* opened fire. The other ships followed. The cannonading consisted of about sixty pieces of cannon. As night came on, Governor Dunmore ordered the boats to burn the warehouses and the wharves, and he hailed Belew to set fire to a large brig which layed at the dock. The other ships in the fleet now sent boats ashore to spread the flames along the river. Since the buildings were chiefly of pine, the conflagration, favored by the wind, spread with amazing rapidity.

"Mothers, with little ones in their arms, were seen by the glare, running through the streets in a shower of cannon balls to get out of range. Two or three were hit. The scene became one of horror and extreme confusion. Several times the British attempted to land with cannon, but were driven back by Howe and Woodford, the American commanders. The cannonading stopped at 10:00 for a short pause, but was renewed. It was kept up until 2:00 the next morning. The flames, which had made their way from street to street and which the American commanders made every effort to arrest, raged for three days until four-fifths of the houses were reduced to ashes.

"The Royal Governor had burned and laid waste the best town in one of England's oldest and most loyal colonies, to which Elizabeth had given her name, Raleigh devoted his fortune, and Shakespeare, Bacon and Herbert tendered a great literary token, a colony where the people had, by themselves, established the national church, and where many were proud that their ancestors had been faithful to the King.

"When Washington heard the fate of his own country, for so he then called Virginia, his breast heaved with waves of anger and grief. 'I hope,' said he, 'this and the threatened devastation of other places will unite the whole country into one indissoluble band against a nation which seems lost to every sense of virtue and those feelings which distinguish a civilized people from the most barbarous savages.' "

Our captain received this news standing on the main deck. He looked out across the harbor, out through the inlet, beyond the breakers, and for the first time in my life I heard him say, "God damn them! They'll pay and they'll pay a thousand fold!"

On the third of January the ladies came aboard, Aunt Kate carrying a package. She stepped with dignity and grace downward from the gangplank and I noticed that she had a slight twinkle in her eye and a turn in the corner of her mouth. She looked me in the eye, but she didn't stare me down, and I must admit I had feelings which I shouldn't have had.

"You are growing up, Alexander," she said as she passed by. She stepped forward to the captain and the ladies lined up at her side. Our men moved forward opposite and behind the captain. Kate unrolled the package and there were two beautiful new flags, the new flags of our country. The captain thanked her most graciously and, losing all of his dignity, he mounted the steps of the poop deck with the alacrity of a young man. In very short order he placed one flag on the jackstaff. The other flag he caressingly folded into a tricone and placed under his arm. He returned slowly and with dignity down the steps, stepped up to Aunt Kate and kissed her on the cheek.

We all descended the gangplank, stood on the dock, and looked at our new flag. Presently the people about the town began to gather and comment on it also. They were pleased with the idea of a new flag, but I was not pleased at all, for to me this flag stood for the same old dilly-dallying, the same old compromise. We were still identified with England by having the crosses in the corner of our flag. Anything would have done if only we had eliminated that British reminder.

I sometimes wondered whether the captain and the members of the crew felt the same way, but they were so grateful to the ladies and so pleased to be able to unfurl a flag and flaunt it in the breeze that all connections with the Crown were for the moment forgotten.

The winter wore on rapidly. The ladies had decided to stay. In the meantime, in the little church in town, our Hessian friend, a very charming fellow, and the English deserter, married the girls of their choice. I heard Captain Hunter remark, "In the absence of the opportunity to bundle, marriage was apt to take place much more rapidly." I knew full well what he meant.

Between keeping the ship in Bristol fashion, working the guns, for we had five now, (four from Sagg Harbour) and occasional hunting, the mild winter went very quickly. Spring was just around the corner when we got the news for which we had been waiting so long.

On the eighteenth of March, 1776, "Privateers were authorized to cruise against ships and their cargoes belonging to any inhabitants of Great Britain, but not of Ireland or the West Indies." We now had our letter of mark.

We took five more men aboard as members of the crew. The first was Howard Hulse, who was signed on as rigger, and the second was Cornelius Irons, a gunner. There was Cornelius Orange, gunner, Ed Hance, boatswain's mate, and William Purchase, designer, rigger, carpenter and general advisor. Mr. Purchase was an old friend of the captain. He had originally migrated with his family from Nova Scotia, and then the old Bay Colony. He had settled on the upper reaches of Barnegat Bay. Mr. Purchase had received the invitation some time before, and had made his way down the Bay, first to Manahawken and then to Little Egg. We were subsequently to wonder how we ever got along without him. Ed Hance was short and stocky, with straight black hair that always needed cutting. He was sincerity down to his finger tips and would have died for any man on the ship. He was also a great sailor and a good rigger. Cornelius Orange and Cornelius Irons were great gunners and big men, both in height and breadth. They were simple and plain Barnegat folk. They saw their duty and did it. Howard Hulse was the real character on the ship. He was signed on not only for his ability as a sailor, having been a waterman along Barnegat Bay for the major portion of his life, but I think the captain also signed him on because of his wild stories. We were a crew of thirteen now,[7] but none of us was superstitious, not even Richard or the local Barnegat Bay men.

Properly rigged, with orders of clearance as a privateer under the twelve colonies of America and the plantation of Georgia, we were now ready to sail. For a 65 foot ship, we were bristling with guns. Every man had at least one pistol and one long arm. There were thirteen swivels mounted at advantageous positions about the deck of the ship. Our brass Rahway cannon pointed out the stern window and our other four guns, heavy iron carronades obtained from the frigate at Sagg Harbour, were lashed to the larboard and starboard sides on the deck, two pointing forward over the sides of the bow.

Having loaded our families and their belongings on the frontier wagon, we started them off with a large convoy and bid them good-bye. The captain was again restless to put to sea, so we all hurried back to our ship. It was still very early in the morning. With a fair wind and a fair tide, we set sail from Little Egg Harbour.

We were now under full sail on another beautiful spring day. I remembered my last walk through the woods. The skunk cabbage was up, the beautiful spirals of the spring ferns were well unfolded and eight or ten inches out of the ground. The willows and the marsh willows were bursting forth in their light green and yellow plumage, and the lavendar maples and Yums glistened in the sunshine.

We sailed through the inlet and on out to sea, into a future no one could imagine or predict—perhaps even death at the end of a hangman's noose on a yardarm of the Jersey.

We sailed straight out to sea, not wishing to get into the sea lane of traffic from England to New York or from England to Philadelphia. The ships in this trade would be large ones and we were yet inexperienced. We wanted to intercept any of the small coastwise ships which generally sail along 15 or 20 miles off the coast. We knew they were most likely Britishers, Loyalists or Tories in the British trade. Although most of our ships had been held in port by the blockade, now, one by one, they would slip out in fog or in the night to become privateers.

Before noon we had lost sight of land. It was a nice day and very clear, so I was sent aloft with a spyglass to search the horizon. I had scarcely raised the glass to my eyes when off to the starboard, coming straight ahead and under full sail, I saw a brig of about 75 tons. I reported to the captain. He called me down and told me to return to the mast with my musket and to keep it out of sight.

Our four deck guns and swivels were covered. To avoid suspicion, we altered our course only slightly so we could pass astern of her. The captain called our men together and told them he would be unable to call them together again because the enemy was undoubtedly looking through their glasses, and although they could not see our preparations now, they soon would. Everything would have to be done in cat fashion, perhaps even to crawling on the deck when the moment came. The fire was lit in the pot on the main deck midships. Fortunately, it gave off no smoke for we were using charcoal instead of cord wood.

In an hour we were very close; in half an hour we were crossing her stern. We waved and they waved back. They hoisted a British flag at the truck. We called, "What ship?" and they replied, "The brig *Greyhound* with a cargo of tea bound for New York."

With that, our captain gave the signal and ran up our Colonial flag. We ran out our guns, opened the window on the stern, and the shiny brass cannon pointed out. As we mounted the swivels, Captain Hunter watched with great interest. The decision was at hand. The captain called to me. "Boy, what do you see?"

"Nothing but confusion, sir. They're not uncovering any guns. They're just whipping more sails on deck. Apparently they intend to run."

Then the captain ordered the gunners "Aim the larboard gun with chain shot and tear it into her rigging."

"Aye, aye, sir," said the gunners and the starboard gun was swung to the larboard, side by side with the larboard gun. The boom and recoil almost set us in stays. I could see the tumbling pair of tied shot rolling through the air.

They went crashing into the mizzenmast and carried away the topsail; down came the rigging to the deck! The brig struck for quarters. "Stand by to go about," cried the captain.

"Aye, aye," was the reply in unison, and one man raised his ramrod.

Our schooner headed over and started to take her first prize. The men now, without command, turned the larboard gun across the deck and lined it up alongside the starboard gun. As we approached cautiously, I unlashed my Lancaster County rifle and brought it to my shoulder. I was determined to be a man and to do a man's work, but I was scared. As we came alongside, I kept my gun levelled at the captain of the brig.

"Tory or Britisher?" shouted the captain.

"I am captain of this ship. I am neither a Britisher nor a Tory. I am loyal to the King. God Save the King!"

Someone in the crew shouted, "God damn the King." It wasn't too popular and it wasn't repeated.

"How many hands aboard?"

"Twelve."

"Send them on deck and lash fast to the side of our ship. Send six men aboard our ship, unarmed!"

"As you wish."

Our captain was stern and precise, and we were proud of him. He ordered the remaining six men to bring all their arms abroad, and the order was obeyed. Our men stood with grim faces, torches in hand, ready to apply them to the fuses on the big, black guns from Sagg Harbor. What a little fellow we were, lashed fast to this big brig. The last six men were next ordered back to sail their ship.

Here we were in our first engagement. We headed back to Little Egg Harbor, loping along at a good speed with our prize. The men who had gone for the guns in the hold of their ship threw them in disgust over to our deck. The captain remonstrated and said if any of them were broken, they would pay for them to the last gun. They passed the remainder across carefully.

Their captain was brought aboard. "If you are a man of honor, I can parole you in your own custody aboard my ship and in the town," said our captain.

"I am a man of honor, Captain Hunter."

We were all surprised and startled. Although we knew that our captain was well known, we didn't know he was that well known.

And so, our captain invited the strange captain, whose name was Vance, to the poop deck where he handed him a box of twists. He sat back and drew a long puff. "Oh, what will my wife say? She told me not to do this, she said I would regret it."

To relieve his mind, our captain said, "Captain, we sail under the articles of war. We're not pirates."

"I'm glad to hear that, Captain Hunter."

"You undoubtedly haven't heard. You were probably at sea when the word came through that after the last horrors, particularly at Portland and Norfolk, we could stand by no longer, so the Continental Congress authorized us in April to sail as privateersmen."

"You have taken a good prize, Captain Hunter. Not only do we have tea aboard, but fifty casks of wine for His Majesty's army in New York."

"If I know the army, they'll certainly miss this wine!" Both captains laughed.

An hour later we saw land and the small chop of white water. This indicated breakers at our inlet. We were safe. Nothing could happen to us now.

How formidable we looked, our men armed to the teeth. Each man, even Richard, carried two pistols. Not only did the captured sailors notice, but the captain of the captured vessel remarked, "This is an exceedingly well trained crew. I'm afraid before it's over you'll raise hell with His Majesty's merchantmen."

We sailed through the inlet and up to the town, our colors flying at the main truck. Someone had turned the Royal Ensign upside down. She was in distress all right. We pulled up to the public dock, but not before the two churches in town tolled their bells until I thought they would burst. The excitement was so great that the town cannon was fired, and all sorts of birds for miles around flew into the sky and disappeared over the horizon or behind the trees. Everyone was running to the wharf. But Captain Vance was still seated on the poop deck, smoking a long, black twist.

The boats were still lashed, side to side. The crew was next marched off to the town jail and Captain Vance was paroled in his own custody within the town limits. He, of course, thought this was a grand gesture. But after all, he knew nothing of this section, for had he ventured 5 or 10 miles—or 15 at the most, in any direction out of town, he would have fallen into the hands of the Barnegat Pirates, the Pine Robbers or the Pine Barons, been stripped of his clothing and left along the road. Our captain was well aware of this.

The town was ours that night. We were the first privateers to venture forth and the first to bring in a prize, but that was only because we had been ready for a long time. Many were still fitting out, changing over, or looking for armament.

Our captain thought it wise to move the brig well up the harbor behind the islands and in among the trees. Then we removed her sails, for they would stand out in contrast against the green of the trees.

At the Customs House, we were given a receipt and her value was placed at $125,000 by the prize court. Our captain requested that an ample amount of this tea be sent on to our general in New York, and that the remainder be distributed throughout the colonies. The wine would be taken care of in the same manner.

After the Customs Prize Court learned that the ship's money consisted of $25,000, almost entirely in gold and silver, and the rest in copper coins, they decided that $12,500 was ours. Our captain assured the judge that we needed no such amount. "We're not pirates," he said. "This money should be sent on to Robert Morris under careful convoy of a mounted militia."

Every remark and movement made by the prize court was passed down the aisle of the Customs House, out through the door and whispered throughout the town to the assembled crowd. As a result, one could not even poach a silver coin, not even for a remembrance. Our captain told the court that five thousand would be ample for us. We had fitted out and paid everything to date. All our men had cast their lots together, and he wanted to reimburse the men and himself to a certain degree. The court tried to raise the amount, but the captain would have no part of it.

Captain Vance, who was present in the court during the entire proceedings, nodded his head and, turning to the crowd, said, "The same honest man, even under the most favorable conditions." He remarked that he should like to write a letter, which could be posted at any place suitable to our captain, but he would not mention our port. However, he wanted it to reach Howe on Staten Island, explaining that his people had received the finest kind of treatment and that it would be exceedingly bad taste to seek any kind of reprisal. The court was adjourned and we all went happily back to our ship. Captain Vance later sailed under our flag and served as a privateersman for us in the Bounty.

Almost daily now other privateers were bringing in their prizes. They were generally small brigs, barks or barkintines, but on rare occasions there were full-rigged ships. These most certainly must have been ships on the high seas before Congress had authorized privateering, ships supplying the British Army and their families, who were billeted in the homes of our brothers and friends in Boston and on Staten Island, where the British army was now camped.[8]

The prizes were coming in daily, and daily the buyers were arriving from Philadelphia and Trenton. These prize articles were sold at auction, and many families who were present with hard money were able to acquire wonderful buys. These prize sales added to the wealth of Egg Harbor, and to the excitement and confusion. It was a constant round of prosperity, and I dare say that many homes in

Philadelphia and throughout central Jersey can still point with pride to purchases from one of these prize courts.

We were living on the fat of the land, so to speak. Everybody was prosperous. We had oyster stews, fried oysters, broiled oysters over open fires, smoked oysters, soft shell crabs, scallops, shrimp cooked in every sort of manner, game and domestic meats, and hickory-smoked rattlesnake.

The inn vied with the cooks at home to tempt the appetite and acquire increased patronage, and we found ourselves eating many meals there. As I found in later life, with prosperity comes fast living, followed by shady women. They were coming to town from distances nearby in the pine belt. It was pitiful to see country girls arrive in their simple garments, then in a short while sailing forth about the town, overly-painted and wearing new silk laces and brocade finery.

Changes were constantly occurring and I was not the only one to observe this, for the members of the crews talked it over. Each time we came in with a prize, we could see a further change in the people and in their manner of living. Everyone was living at a faster pace and the people were becoming harder. The country draft horse was no longer satisfactory for pulling the carriage or country wagon. Now light, fast horses were required. The people were dressing more elaborately all the time and, although we read in the newspapers and heard from the Liberty Boys and circuit riders of the intense suffering of our army, these people were going on as though they were living in another world.

I had heard my father say when I was a boy that great changes came over the seaport towns in New England as the whaling industry became a great oil monopoly. Now I was seeing it all over again. It was particularly distressing to see the drunken women and hear their raucous laughter. Most of our younger men spent as much time ashore as possible and came aboard during the wee hours. They were on the job at a moment's notice, however, and I must say that none of our crew displayed themselves in public in a disgraceful manner, or ever came aboard with too much drink.

The captain had been waiting for the new edition of the newspaper, the *Gazetteer*, and it finally arrived. We hoisted sail and left our little town behind, passing through the inlet of Little Egg for the third time.

We sailed straight out to sea again about 25 miles. Knowing that the British fleet would be approaching New York at this season of the year, since the Howes were on Staten Island, we decided to proceed southward because there were a number of shallow inlets which would afford us protection in the back bays. If necessary, we could sail behind the islands and eventually reach our home port without being seen. Of course, sailing in the back bays was a dangerous thing for a small ship with so small a crew. The Pine Barons might try to take us, for their bands were very large, their organization was good, and they respected no one. They had no more use for the Loyalists and the Tories than they had for us, the so-called Rebels. They had no more use for the Quakers than they did for the Barnegat Pirates. These Pine Robbers and the so-called Pine Barons, their leaders, lived by what they obtained from the murder of unfortunate travelers. Although there is no record that the Barnegat Pirates ever attacked the Pine Robbers, there are ever so many records of the Pine Barons and their bands attacking the Barnegat Pirates.

These Pine Robbers would attack a wagon train or a caravan, slay the men, rape and then murder the women, and carry off the plunder and loot. Then the leaders, dressed in the finest linens, silks, satins, brocades, and wool clothes adorned with gold buckles, would go in their fine wagons drawn by excellent horses and sell this plunder in Philadelphia, masking as traveling merchants. They would state that their goods had just come into Little Egg and were transported at great expense and speed to the city of Philadelphia in order that they could have the fine things in time for the fall season and the balls.

Barnegat Pirates would destroy a ship on the beach and remove the cargo, only to be killed by the Pine Barons and Robbers, who would then appropriate the cargo.

At any rate, the many inlets below Little Egg offered us a haven in time of need. A fight with these robbers was more desirable than a noose around the neck and swingling from the King's yardarm.

We sailed lazily all that day and the following day down the coast. At night we sailed without lights or with the curtains drawn in the captain's cabin and the fo'c's'l.

On the following morning just before daybreak, I was suddenly awakened by the violent shaking of my arm. Mr. Irons told me to get up and get up quickly. I heard the men above rushing about and I flew on deck in only my breeches. The sun was just appearing beyond the horizon and there standing off our bow on the larboard side, within gun shot, was a large ship carrying the British flag. She was loping along slowly in the opposite direction. There was considerable excitement aboard our ship, because we were each within range of the other. She was headed toward New York.

Almost before we could turn, many men were coming on her deck and leaning over the rail. I was then sent aloft again. Her men must have been wondering what such a small ship would be doing out here and what our intentions were. To our great surprise, she allowed us to pass and, although they waved, they did not hail us. I believe they were suspicious, but they made no attempt to intercept us.

We altered our course quickly and the captain asked, "Boy, what do you see?"

"They're uncovering guns, sir. I count six guns, three on a side."

"Watch the poop deck, boy. See if they uncover a gun on the stern."

"There is no gun on her poop deck, sir."

"Then watch the stern window for a gun."

"Yes, sir. But I still see no gun!" By this time we were

sailing across her stern. Automatically, the gunners had rolled the two great iron guns to the larboard side.

"Aim one chain shot at her mizzen rigging, men. Aim the other gun right into her counter ... when you're ready, let her go. They can't possibly hit us, for they have no stern gun. We'll slacken sail just enough to give you a better chance to aim."

The torches were brought from the pot and the fuses ignited. The two great carronades from the British frigate at Sagg Harbor went off, one after the other. The pound was deafening as they vomited fire. It shook our little ship and the guns recoiled on their lanyards like angry dragons. The first shot hit her square on the counter. The second tore through the top of the mizzen and into the rigging of the mainmast. I could see the chained balls spin round and round as they tore through the mass of stays.

"Captain, shall we try hot shot?" cried Mr. Irons.

"No, Cornelius. We haven't had enough experience with hot shot and I don't want anything to happen at a time like this. The odds are too great as it is. We probably should have run. We'll make one more pass at her. Let's go downwind a little so we keep to her stern. Boy, watch and see that they don't uncover a gun on the poop deck."

"Sir, they couldn't get a gun up on the poop deck. It's too high above the main."

"Very good, boy," replied the captain.

At the sails were John Hunter, Fred Sykes, and Mr. Pearsall. Howard Hulse stood by the main sail as the Springers handled the wheel with great skill.

"Can you swing the gun as we go about?"

"Aye, aye, sir," spoke up the six men at the guns.

Now Richard came on deck with Ed Hance and William Purchase. This made nine men on the two guns. As we went downwind and went about smartly, our guns were reversed and again we sailed across her stern and into range. She had no stern gun all right. "Poor helpless bastards," muttered Ed Hance. But their men were firing their small arms and trying to work her around to give us a broadside.

"Boom!" went our two guns again. The smoke and fire belched forth enveloping our little ship. We again veered off and sailed away on an angle, remaining to the stern of this great ship. One of our shots fell short in the excitement; we had failed to put in the required amount of powder. But the other shot was apparently just right, for it crashed through the stern window above the counter and smoke soon began to rise.

We had exposed something. She was now afire in the stern and down came her colors. We proceeded cautiously up to her stern, both our other guns pointed off the starboard and larboard quarters forward. We asked her name and compliment of the crew. We had so defaced her nameboard we couldn't recognize her port or name.

There were 24 men in the crew. We covered them with our muskets and our captain ordered them to attack the fire. He ordered the captain and officers to stand at attention on the poop deck, right over the fire. They showed considerable concern. I kept my Long Tom trained on the captain from my position in the maintop.

Richard, who couldn't hit the broad side of a Pennsylvania barn, had a blunderbuss at his waist. I don't believe it was even loaded. But he wore a very mean, savage expression and in this manner held the three senior officers at bay.

In about half an hour the fire was under control and our captain ordered twelve men aboard our ship. We sent them below and locked them up. Then we lashed alongside, putting their remaining men to work clearing the rubble and chopping away the mizzen we had destroyed. We set off immediately for the coast, knowing full well that we were in a dangerous situation in transatlantic lanes.

On the way in, we luckily met two other ships, one a schooner and one a brig, both out of Egg Harbor, and they escorted us in. We felt greatly relieved from so great a responsibility. Amid cheers and hurrahs, we entered the harbor at sunset with our big prize. As we did so, the captain heaved a great sigh of relief, for the wind was dying. He ordered the captured sailors from the ship to lower their long boat and released the twelve men from below decks. They lowered the gig, attached the boats to our ship and, heaving at the oars and with the aid of a dying wind, we finally at dark, reached the public dock.

Within twenty minutes, the church bells began to peal and pandemonium broke loose again. Under torch light and lantern, the dock was filled with people, this time with ladies of the evening. Only with the aid of the militia were we able to keep them off our ship.

The "prize" crew was marched to the jail and the captain with them, but not before our captain had taken possession of his official records.

The ship was the *Dolly Martin* from Nantucket, originally in the whale trade. She had sailed from Philadelphia loaded with furniture, beds, muskets and powder for the Loyalists on Staten Island and New York, uniforms for the new Loyalist regiment which was to be recruited in northern New Jersey, Staten Island, Long Island, New York, and lower Westchester. She carried $36,000 in gold and $5,000 in silver. She also carried corned beef and sauerkraut, new potatoes and good old Philadelphia beer. And she had 50 barrels of bourbon whiskey, fine Pennsylvania frontier bourbon whiskey, 50 barrels of wine, and 25 barrels of cider, which I assume was hard. I knew damn well that all this liquor would not reach our army and our people. Little Egg would be wilder than it had ever been.

We received our prize money, although we insisted on only taking five thousand dollars. We saw that the rest was sealed in an iron strong box to be sent on to Robert Morris. I couldn't help but feel that either it takes an awful lot of money to run a war, or there must be somebody along the line dipping into the box.

We all walked down the street together, the officers filing along with the captain. I walked behind the officers, followed by the crew. The complimentary taunts and pleadings of the street women were difficult to refuse. But we marched with heads not too high, returning an occasional smile or remark, for we did not wish to gain the enmity of these people. Finally we reached our ship. As we walked aboard, we wondered what had happened to the captain. He seemed unusually serious.

"Sit down, men. I'd like to talk to you. The manner in which all of you conducted yourselves these past two weeks saved us from irons, the prison ship Jersey and the hangman's noose. I subjected you men to an unnecessary risk. We had ample opportunity to run away from this last great ship and we could easily have escaped. She was a lumbering old whaler, but like the beautiful women we should run from and don't, so here we should have run but didn't. She was deep in the water and full in the bow, as all whalers are. She was slow, cumbersome and difficult to turn around. We, of course, can almost spin on a penny. However I subjected you to the risk. If she had had the brains to place a big gun out of her stern quarter, with a crew of good gunners aboard, she could have blown us out of the water. That's how great the risk was! We depended upon the good eyes of this boy to watch for that maneuver. The minute he saw her roll out a gun, our only hope would have been to fly off on the quarter tack and zigzag. We could not have gotten out of her range quickly because we couldn't sail fast enough. But perhaps we could have sailed out of her aim.

"It so happens that we have some great gunners aboard this ship, and I can't compliment them too highly. The element of surprise was too great for that crew. They had twenty-four men and six guns and they soon knew we were vastly superior to them in experience. You noticed that was a very tough looking crew, but they didn't have a chance to fight."

"We were even lucky with the tide and the amount of sea running," I injected.

"I never thought of the tide, men," said the captain. "Just think if we had tried to sail thru this inlet at low tide with that ship. We would have grounded her and blocked this inlet. That might have been fatal for us."

"Not at all, Captain," said Mr. Sykes. "If we had grounded her, the smaller boats would have gone aboard and stripped her, or she would have floated with the next tide. As it is, we've set up an enviable record, Captain, a record other privateersmen can follow."

"That's just the trouble, Mr. Sykes. I'm afraid we'll all reach too far. It's just occurred to me, men, that we haven't eaten since morning. Let's go down, give Richard a hand, and get something to eat."

Richard had disappeared down the companionway steps and, as we filed down, the meal was already in preparation. We ate and drank. I drank a Madeira wine from the first prize ship and was it good! The captain looked at me, I thought a little sadly. "Boy, you're growing up."

Everyone was in a talkative mood so we talked for hours. We talked about our next adventures and I asked the captain about the Barnegat Pirates.

"That's right, my boy, I never have told you about the Barnegat Pirates. But before I do that, I want to caution you about the pirates out on that dock. They, too, are Barnegat Pirates. Stay away from them. A moment's satisfaction may be followed by years of suffering and regret. A woman who cavorts with one man out of wedlock will cavort with any other. Some day unexpectedly, perhaps in the strangest port far from home, you will suddenly meet the girl of your dreams, the girl of your fondest hopes. You will know it when it happens and you will only experience it once in a lifetime. There will be no running from it and it might even cause you to jump ship to be with her."

"Nothing would ever make me jump ship, Captain."

"I hope not, but I think every man on this boat will bear me out in what I've said."

I looked around to see what the other men thought and saw the men nodding, one by one. Yet I had suspicions that many of them left the boat late at night and returned early in the morning.

"Now for the Barnegat Pirates! I believe the name originally came from a group of people who operated from the lower end of Monmouth County, at the Squan River, down to Barnegat Inlet. These people must operate in a locality not too far from known lighthouses. As you know, there's a light on Sandy Hook Island. I believe the light was established in 1713. There's also a light located on the south side of Barnegat Inlet. But since, in coastwise trade, so many ships have been piling up for years along that beach, a number of lights have been established along the coast.

"The second condition they require to operate is a desolate, forlorn country, far from good roads leading into the interior, and far away from any means of communication. So after these pirates wreck a ship, they're able to scatter before word reaches the capital and militia can be dispatched to intercept them.

'A third condition necessary for their successful operation is bad weather. They operate best at night, in storms, or in snow storms, light flurries and high seas. As the dirty weather approaches, they collect great piles of driftwood on the beach and set it afire after dark. They place a horse or mule beyond the fire, put on a long blanket that just about touches the ground, then march this horse or mule around the fire at a steady pace, in order to give the impression of a light flashing on and off. Thinking this is an inlet and a lighthouse, this attracts a ship toward the beach. In the case of Barnegat Inlet, the captain of the ill-fated ship, assuming that the light is on the south side of the inlet, allows ample distance, five or six hundred feet to the north of the light. Then, to his dismay, he comes crashing onto the beach. In a short while he piles up on the shoals and the ship begins to break up. Or if it doesn't break up by morning, if the seas have abated, these pirates put out in boats through the surf and bring the people off. When they've brought them ashore, they butcher them for their jewels, clothing, and money. They either cast them back into the sea or bury them in shallow graves.

"Women receive the same treatment as men. There's a little spot on the coast, which you may see on your maps, called Ship's Bottom. It is reputed that a Spanish vessel, before the revolution, cruising in trade off the coast, was forced ashore here in a January storm. It broke up during the night, the people floated ashore, and they were treated in the manner I just described. Days and days later, when the militia reached the beach and all was calm and serene, the ship had heeled up its bottom, but then someone heard a cry and a pounding. Eight militiamen reached the side of the derelict, punched a hole in the side, and a beautiful Spanish lady, not much the worse for her experience, stepped into the surf boat. She was the only known survivor of the Barnegat Pirates. Thus the name, Ship's Bottom."

"Whose side are they on, Captain," I said.

"They are on no one's side except the side of the devil, lad. No one knows who they are. Some of them may live right here in Little Egg. At the upper end of Barnegat Bay, back about half a mile from the ocean on the north side of the inlet, is an old rambling farmhouse, not far from a little fresh water lake. I have been in that house many times, for I have sailed in and out of that old inlet at the north end of Barnegat Bay on many occasions. I have carried poeple to New York and to the capital at Perth Amboy. I have been wined and dined in that old farmhouse,* and I'm sure that much of the plate and silver, and much of the fine furniture, drapes and fine rugs was part of loot obtained in this manner. I'm certain I've seen salt water stains on some of the rugs. I'm certain that the owner and his friends are engaged in Barnegat pirating."

Someone said, "That's as good as a ghost story, Captain." The captain beamed.

"Thank you very much," I said.

"You're welcome, my boy, and speaking of ghosts, the more important thing to remember is to stay away from these phantoms out on the dock. But speak kindly to them if you're spoken to, and talk kindly to all the people around town, no matter how queer they may seem to you.

---

*Now Bayhead, N. J.

We can't afford to make any enemies in this locality. Their jealousy may become very great and we may even have to change our port. I have seen no evidence of it yet, but it may come."

Mr. Irons spoke up and assured the captain that we were well liked and greatly respected.

"I hope that will continue, Mr. Irons."

We laid in port for several days, holystoning the deck, adjusting our rigging, and painting the ship. The next morning we repaired the sails, strengthened, repaired and replaced lines, halyards and stays. The gunners practiced with the guns, for they were very proud of their work and their big black carronades. They were proud of their accomplishments and were determined to improve in the future. We now had ample powder with which to practice. I took part in all kinds of tasks from the top of the mast to the bottom of the ship, even inspecting for imaginary leaks along the keel.

I noticed that as time went on, the captain's countenance grew more worried. On a number of occasions I heard him telling Mr. Sykes and Mr. Pearsall that our luck couldn't possibly hold out forever, that the day would come when we would certainly meet our match. Too many prizes were being brought into Little Egg, so that if nothing else happened before the cold weather, the British were bound to come down, sack the town, and burn the ships. He felt that we all should take greater care watching for strange ships, and the road through the pines should be closely guarded, to prevent the infiltration of spies.

At the end of about a week, we were ready to sail. But that night, before sunset, there was a particularly low-hanging series of grey clouds completely enveloping the horizon. The sea birds were flying in even greater numbers and the land birds were very quiet. The wind had been exceedingly unsteady for several days, first blowing from one quarter and then another, then completely boxing the compass and finally dying. There had been an unusually high series of tides, although there was not a full moon.

This worried the captain, for he knew there were violent disturbances at sea and he was desirous of seeking a more suitable anchorage. He felt certain we were in for a hurricane. The question was, what would the direction be? If the direction was from the land, it might be desirable to lay behind Tucker Island, as far away from flying branches as possible, or across the bay close to the trees. On the other hand, if the storm was coming from the sea, it wouldn't be the first time the seas had come over Tucker Island, and the anchorage there would be unsafe. The ship might pull her anchors, drift across the bay and be destroyed on a leeward shore.

All the men stood on the poop deck, surveying the harbor. Finally they all decided we would lay in a little twisting creek about a mile away from the pines and about two miles from Tucker Island. This was far enough away from the pines to be out of the reach of any possible night attack by the Pine Robbers ... or even the Loyalists or refugees, as they were sometimes called. At the same time, regardless of how high the tide might be, we would be protected, for there were many large willow trees with deep taproots along the bank, and to protect our ship, we could throw out lines to these trees.

And so we upped anchor and sailed up the bay and into our little creek. We faced our bow toward Parker Island in the east. During the night, the tide continued to rise unusually high and the wind increased in violence. We were rocking and rolling, even in this little creek. By morning, the wind had increased to most violent proportions. There wasn't a sign of a bird in the air and the dome of the sky, down to the horizon, was completely circled by great lead-colored clouds. There was no sight of the miles of marsh. The willows were now standing deep in water, and the wind and gusts were so violent that they screeched through our rigging. The boats in the harbor were pitching, plunging, yawing, and dashing, and some had either broken their cables or pulled their moorings, and were across on the lee shore, being destroyed by enormous waves.

One apparently struck a large submerged stump and sunk almost to its deck. The seas, coming across the bay, were breaking in the rigging. There wasn't a sign of a person on the street, and one or two houses had lost their roofs. The wind pulled the shingles off the others like the plucking of a chicken. I realized how comfortable I had been during the night between my two feather ticks.

The great wind was picking up the water, particularly in its gusts, chopping it off the tops of the crests of the waves, and throwing it through the air in solid sheets of water. When it struck, it was enough to cut your face. It was utterly impossible to look into the wind or face these seas. The bay was a steaming, boiling, cauldron of white water. The odor of the sea was everywhere, and across the bay came great sheets of driving rain. How happy I was that there were two anchors out on the bow, one on the stern, and four side lines going to the great willow trees. I had the feeling that a swamp willow was built for this very purpose. Although they were bent over like the ostrich plumes on a cockade, they would hold. The wind now howled fiercely, moaning and whistling through the rigging. At times it sounded like Negro spirituals afar off on a warm summer night. But this was not a warm summer day; it was late September and the wind was cold and vicious. The mercury in the glass tube continued to fall so fast that by very close scrutiny, you could almost see it going down.

One of the men standing on the companionway stairs cried out, "There go two more ships across the bay. Their lines just parted. Look at 'em go!" One shortly fetched up on a shoal which, before the storm, had been an island. The other seemed to sail right on by, but just when it was almost clear, it struck and swung, as its stern crashed into the bow of the first one, tearing away part of the counter on the second ship. Then she continued on at great speed across the bay and ended up on the shore among the trees. The topmast of other ships were flying off and crashing down upon other decks, held together only by their stays. The tops of the trees on the edge of the forest were ripping off and flying through the air. The wind played through our rigging, moaning and groaning in a melancholy dirge. The seas now completely covered the dock and the main wharf of the town, and the waterfront streets were now under water.

Water continued to crash against the waterfront buildings and presently the sides of one of the warehouses collapsed. The roof fell and soon both were floating off in the raging, roaring water across the bay. Between the puffs, we could see the great waves in the ocean mount and cover over Tucker Island, cutting down the lower portions of the dunes, particularly toward the tip at the north side of the island. I prayed that our little ship would hold, or we would be hopelessly consumed. How silly of me to worry about Pine Robbers and Pine Barons, Loyalists, and Barnegat Pirates!

The top of the steeple of one of the two churches now sailed through the air like a great dart. It disappeared somewhere on the west side of town with a consuming crash. The storm was coming in from the southeast.

I went into the captain's cabin where he and the mates were talking and smoking their pipes. Mr. Pearsall was smoking a long, black twist and they were discussing similar storms in the past. They all agreed that this was the worst one they had ever seen. I was amazed at their calmness. The rain banged and crashed on the poop deck over our heads, a solid avalanche of water. The seas smashed against the sides and Richard sat in the corner of the galley, his Bible on his lap. Between his praying, he repeated, ' The fishes wool make a fuss over me."

The captain, recognizing his fright, said, "Richard, you're safer here than any other place in this area, safer than on shore and far safer than in a house, because this little ship is built for just what it is going through." Richard immediately seemed to feel better, but I wasn't so sure. I was still frightened. I couldn't help but think how utterly terrifying it would be at sea in such a storm. How glad I was that we were in Parker's Creek.

With that the captain turned to the mates. "I believe it's letting up. Apparently we were in the direct line of the storm and the first half has passed over. We're now in the center. There'll be a lull followed by a return and an increase in the violence. As the last of the outside of the circle passes over us, it will be worse."

The day was wearing away; we went up on deck. The ship was pitching and rocking violently. Even the experienced mates and the captain looked with as much consternation at what they saw as I did. The town was a shamble; both church steeples were gone and at least a dozen houses had lost their roofs. The seas were well up in the streets fronting the bay. Two wharf buildings were completely gone and we could see people wandering aimlessly on the upper street of the town back from the bay. A large number of ships were across the bay on the western shore, battered, beaten and crashed together. One ship was over on its side and sunk. The other, a little ship which had been sunk before, was completely underwater with only the mast sticking out.

We checked our lines. The willows and anchors were holding, but the tops of the trees on the western shore were blown off in many places, and many trees were completely uprooted and underwater. The seas were still crashing wildly across the greater part of Tucker Island.

The ocean beyond the inlet was boiling like the bay, but so far away it was difficult to tell how bad it really was. The bay was filled with floating barrels, boxes, wagons, and, I'm sorry to say, the carcasses of animals. Little skiffs and whale boats were floating everywhere. We inspected our rigging, but everything seemed in good order. The wind was again increasing in violence. Darkwater, an indication of the second part of the hurricane, was now slanting across the bay and the captain shouted, ' Down below!"

We dashed down the companionway steps and slammed the hatch door just as it hit. With the first blast, we careened and fetched up on our lines. Our staunch little ship creaked from her masthead to her keel and she began to pitch violently. The rain came down as though the skies had emptied and the seas crashed against our sides. I felt short of breath, hungry for air, grabbed hold of the table and took deep breaths.

Darkness from the storm, and the approaching darkness of the end of day added to the somberness. The whale oil lamps were lit and hurricane glasses were placed over them. Even with this protection, each great blast of wind would dim the lights. They would flicker and almost go out. In the lull, the light in the lamps would triumphantly rise and dissipate the shadows.

Richard's fears became so great that he moved off into the corner and began to pray aloud. The captain took out his Bible and read: "Good Lord, from the perils of the sea, deliver us!" It helped Richard but not me. I thought of home, so snug and sweet, of my mother and the farm.

It was no use trying to keep a fire in the fireplace; it just wouldn't burn. In the cold and semidarkness, we ate a little leftover food. Now we sat around with very little conversation and gradually, one by one, filed off to bed. For some little time, even snug between my feather beds, I rolled and pitched violently, but I was not sick and eventually I fell off to sleep.

The next morning I awakened early and was astonished at the silence. The bay was tranquil and there was the pungent smell of the sea. I dressed quickly and went up on deck, where I was all alone beneath an overcast sky. I began to look around.

The havoc was indescribable. A huge white wall of water replaced the inlet. A continuous bombardment of the town by the entire British fleet could never have produced the destruction seen on both land and sea. The boom of the surf on the far side of the dunes was as frightening as Indian drums in the forest at night. Most of the fleet was on the lea shore, destroyed into a jumbled mass of timber, rigging and uprooted trees. Some of the boats had actually crashed against the trees, high on the land well beyond the marsh. Others were in the forest among the trees. The water had receded somewhat and the contours of the island and the creek were beginning to take form. The water was rushing by toward the inlet at breakneck speed. Most of the whale boats which had survived were being carried out to sea.

The rain had stopped and people were appearing in the town and upon the decks of the surviving ships. The seas were still crashing against Tucker Island, sounding like the boom of distant battle, the white spray going straight skyward and drenching the island. Rivulets of water were coming across between the low areas and between the dunes.

The rest of our crew soon came on deck. Our damage was negligible, but as I looked over the side, I saw that our fresh paint was pretty badly scarred. As the day wore on, the bay returned to normal. The glass was now rising and the wind returned to a gentle westerly. The land birds were still absent, but the water fowl were returning to the bay. It didn't seem possible that nature could be so cruel and now so calm.

Although the tide was still high, one wharf was out of water and intact. We placed a man on the bow to watch for floating wreckage, hoisted sail, freed our lines, pulled up our anchors and sailed across to the remaining wharf where we docked. The wharf was worse for wear, yet still in a safe condition. We went ashore, at the captain's suggestion, to help the townspeople.

The town was a shambles. Window frames were blown out, the militia was on the street, and shopkeepers were gathering up lumber to board up their windows. Some people still wandered aimlessly in fear and anxiety for their loved ones. Others walked as though in a daze. There were no signs of the fancy ladies now; they had all fled.

We worked hard through the following days and gradually the town took on some appearance of being normal. It was voted by the prize court that some money from the next prize should be given to the unfortunates to pay for their losses. Whale boats were now starting across the bay to determine the damage and offer what help they could give to the ships cast upon the beach on the western shore. As bodies were recovered in the town and from the wrecked ships, carts brought them in. For days on end there was a continuous procession to the local cemetery at the edge of town.

We all wrote letters home, and put them in the postal box at the inn. We were anxious for our families to know how well we were and how little we had actually suffered. In my letter, I begged for news from home. I'm quite sure the rest of the men did the same. Richard was still frightened and to relieve him from work, we all ate at the inn.

Day after day stories came in of heroism on land and aboard ships in the bay. No ships came in through the inlet, so there was no news from the outside. Armed people walked the beaches with a mounted militia detachment to prevent looting by the Barnegat Pirates. Fortunately, no ships had been driven ashore on the ocean beaches.

# 5

*By the beginning* of November, we had turned our efforts to repainting and refitting our little vessel, and on the fifteenth of November, in a calm sea and on a mild day, we sailed forth to new adventure. We hadn't traveled more than 15 miles when we came upon a great ship, one of the great prizes of the war and one of the richest, the ship *Venice* from London.

We approached it in the usual cautious manner, without hoisting a pennant or a flag. When we were within hailing distance, we found that she was not armed, and so we took her without incident. The affair had so little drama that when we sailed into Little Egg, we turned her over to the prize court at once and since the day was still young, we sailed right out again. We later learned that the *Venice* had left London long before Benjamin Franklin's warning that "unless the King modified his attitude, we would arm and go to sea."

We sailed down the coast toward Delaware Bay and the following morning we sighted another square-rigged ship, loping along in a lazy manner. We hailed her and found it to be the *Major Pearson* heading from London to Philadelphia. We asked her what armament she carried and her captain replied, "What armament? We are not a man of war, we are a merchantman! What are you, a pilot boat?"

The blood vessels stood out on the captain's forehead. "A pilot boat!" I could see his face turn scarlet and he whispered half under his breath, "The damn fools!"

Grabbing a trumpet, he called across the narrow expanse of water, "We are a privateer of the American Colonial navy. We are well armed and we suggest you strike your colors at once."

"The hell you say!" returned the Britisher.

Either by design or excitement, Mr. Irons swung the lighted torch in a great circle and amid shouts of "Hurrah," he struck the fuse on the cannon and there was a terrific boom! The ball crashed the great merchantman amidships, carrying away a section of the rail, the belaying pin rack (fife rail) and bringing down the yardarm of the mainsail, the lower maintopsail, the upper maintopsail and the topgallant. I never saw a ship strike her colors faster. Our men rolled on the deck in laughter and our captain, his hands on the rail, looked into the water and smiled.

And so, the *Major Pearson,* bound from London to Philadelphia, came into the port of Little Egg. We had captured two of the richest prizes of the war, returning to Little Egg three days from the time we had left.

After we were safe, within the harbor, our captain said, "It'll never happen again. . . .it'll never happen again. Something terrible lies ahead. I have a premonition, but I can't tell what it is. I don't know."

The town went wild. The little privateers that had survived the storm, even with their dirth of powder, fired one shot. It was a holiday occasion all right. To avoid embarrassment and to belittle our importance, we decided to put to sea at once, but we were restrained by the townspeople. That night at the inn there was a great dinner, speeches, beautiful red-eyed women, and many compliments for our captain, his crew, and our gallant little ship. The sincerity of our new friends was really astounding. Of course, these were not all local people, for Little Egg was the greatest rendezvous for privateers during the war.

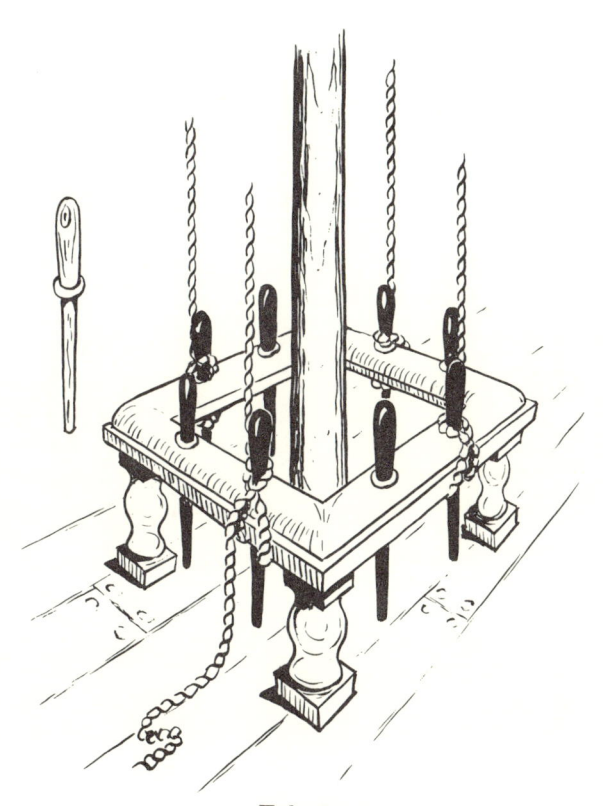

*Fife Rail*

*Plan of Action against a large ship*

While some captains were dancing, others were walking about, bowing and nodding to the ladies. I was smoking a twist and I had a glass of wine. I don't know whether it was the twist or the wine, but I was soon feeling very queer. Suddenly a courier burst into the banquet room. The music stopped as he mounted the platform.

"I have just come from New York. The British are sending a fleet to Little Egg to destroy the town and hang you all on the yardarm of the Jersey without trial. The British generals at Staten Island are infuriated because their merchant ships and transports have been seized and destroyed by the privateers in this 'rat's nest,' as they call it. They're determined to destroy it and they're on their way now."*

The meeting broke up at once. The people returned in panic to their homes and the militia went off to set up their defense. The sailors returned to their ships and, not wanting to wait for the morrow and the possibility of surprise, we decided to go through the inlet that night. It was dark as we started through the inlet, then suddenly the bow watch cried, "There are a great number of lights ahead! They appear to be from ships of the line."

Someone in the crew cried out, "My God, they're here!" They were here all right.

"Stand by to go about," cried the captain. Grabbing the wheel, he threw her hard over and sailed her back to the town and tied up at the wharf. He sent dispatchers throughout the town, telling the people that the British were outside the inlet waiting for dawn. This would give them some time to escape the hangman's noose or the end of a saber or bayonet. We then proceeded to sail slowly up the bay, behind the islands, along the fresh ground, feeling our way without lights with raised centerboard. When we thought we were a safe distance from any ship that might have followed us in the dark, yet well out from shore, safe from Barnegat Pirates or Pine Robbers, we laid to for the night.

---

*From The Rivington Press, New York Town.

No one slept that night. We all were on watch, armed to the teeth for the Pine Robbers as well as the British.

In the morning, we saw townspeople fleeing across the bay and marshes on boats, rafts and even logs. The British expedition consisted of ten vessels and about four hundred men. The flagship was the *Zebra*. We could see through our glasses the ships coming into the harbor. They were small ships. Had we only known or had we had some kind of organization, we could have whipped the stuffing out of them and taken them all as prizes. There wasn't a single ship of the line in the lot. My God, what a disappointment!

In the meantime, General Washington, hearing of this expedition, dispatched Count Pulaski and his legion. At the same time, he sent a warning to Tuckerton in time for the privateers and people to escape. Pulaski arrived at Tuckerton three days after the British had landed and left.

We now decided to sail down the bay and go to sea through the lower inlet. As we did so, we could see Egg Harbour burning, particularly Chestnut Neck on the Mullacca River. Then we saw ten or twelve houses on Bass River and Tucker's Mill burning. There were about thirty prize vessels lying in the harbor and the British set them all afire.

The British boats and troops retired and landed at Osborne's Island, four miles west of Tuckerton, during the night. They captured a sentinel and compelled him to lead them to the spot where Pulaski's picket guard was stationed. The guard consisted of about thirty men. Surprised by the enemy, every one of them was put to death. The British quickly returned to their ships, tearing up the Quaker Bridge as they went to prevent Pulaski from overtaking them. As the enemy fleet was going over the bar, the *Zebra* grounded and, to prevent her falling into the hands of the Americans, they set her afire. As the fire reached her guns, they discharged, much to the amusement of the Americans who were watching.

With General Pulaski's legion close at hand, the British were reluctant to pursue those who had fled to the back bay behind the islands. Meanwhile, we reversed our course before reaching the lower inlet, and sailed back into Little Egg.

The conflagration was horrible. The acrid stench of fire and smoke was everywhere, and there had been tremendous destruction. Before the British arrived, the town had scarcely recovered from the hurricane and now, on top of all this, we had lost our two great prizes. However, we had fortunately salvaged the goods beforehand and sent the money to Robert Morris. The British had burned thirty-two ships and the entire town, but most of our privateers had escaped into the back bay. The factories, the shipyards, the remaining warehouses, even the cemetery, had all been destroyed. Little Egg was gone forever.

It was growing very cold now and all evidence pointed to a long, hard winter. All the privateersmen held a meeting, for since we were so close to New York, our privateers were still in danger. Thus we decided to change our operations to the south. The British were getting ready to put into operation their master plan of separating the South from the Middle Atlantic colonies and, in turn, the middle from the New England colonies. In view of this, our captain, who was familiar with that part of the country, particularly the shores and waters of the Chesapeake Bay, decided to sail south.

And so, after having provisioned our little craft as best we could, we set sail on the first of December, 1777, thirty privateers in a grand parade. We decided no matter what happened, we would all stick together.

The last of the ducks and geese were going south now. Only small covies of mallards remained. That meant it was very cold in Boston, Gloucester and out on Nantucket. We had seen signs in the coats of freshly killed deer, the coats of woodchuck, squirrel and muskrat. Everyone agreed, ashore and afloat, that the coat of the animals was unusually heavy this year.

Our decision turned out to be a wise one for, due to the cold, the British in New York went into winter quarters early. We heard that our army was suffering on the outskirts of New York at Kingsbridge, while we were comfortable, with plenty to eat and drink and plenty of cord wood for our fireplace. As we sailed down the coast in the cold of those December days, I had ample opportunity to find out about many things.

One lovely afternoon, as our ship rose and fell in a fine quarter sea and the men were sitting about the deck resting and chatting, the conversation lagged. I said, "Captain, what do you mean when you speak of bundling?"

For a moment he looked surprised, and then the surprise shifted to embarrassment. After a deep breath, he stared out across the water and began.

"In the early days of the colonies, the houses were apt to be far apart, except where they were clustered in little towns or hamlets. When a fellow came a-courting, particularly during the winter months, he was apt to be forced to stay all night. In bad weather, he might leave home well before dark and reach the young lady's home long after dark. To venture home in the snow, a long distance late at night, was extremely hazardous, for in the early days the wolves roved our country in packs. The lack of wealth among the farmfolk, together with their frugality, caused them to build small compact houses which were easier to heat. When the weather became very cold and courting was in earnest, a poster bed was set up in the living room with a fireplace and a well-laid fire. And when the future groom arrived, both girl and boy would sit up in the bed with a centerboard between them, bundled under the heavy covers, and they would talk and plan their future far into the cold night. Then at daybreak, the groom-to-be would be on his way. Sometimes the house had a single daughter's wing.

"There's a humorous little tale always told around the firehouses about a young boy and girl, fifteen or sixteen years old. It seems that the girl and her family were visiting the family of the boy. A very bad storm came up and they were forced to stay overnight. Having arranged the center-

*Single Daughter's Wing, 1700*

board, the parents proceeded to put the two children into bed. The next day the two children were walking down the road and they came to a nut tree behind a low stone wall. The little girl remarked, 'I like hickory nuts,' and the little boy replied, 'I'll go over the wall and get some for you.' She returned with scorn, 'You can never get over that wall if you couldn't even get over the centerboard last night!'" We all looked at the captain in surprise; some men slapped their knees and roared.

"On other occasions, the mother would sew her daughter's nightclothes, front and back, and then examine the garment very thoroughly in the morning." I must have looked surprised, for he said, "Son, I don't want you to look with scorn upon this custom because these were economic necessities. It takes time to cut cordwood and wood burns rapidly. People must court in order to raise families in order to people this great nation. And if a boy and girl were to sit side by side on a horsehair sofa or a hard chair all evening in the cold, and then the boy was turned out into the howling weather and in the dark to go home, I'm afraid there would have been much less courting, fewer marriages and fewer people." Our captain could explain all sorts of customs in the simplest way.

As agreed, the little fleet was keeping close together, for when one boat would start to outrun another, that boat would slacken sail until the other had closed its distance.

On the morning of the third day, off the coast of Delaware, we picked up two of His Majesty's ships bound for the Delaware. They had been driven southward slightly off their course by storm, poor seamanship and poor navigation. We boarded them, took their supplies and money and divided them among our ships. Then we divided their arms. They signed the book that they were prizes and we ordered them to follow us.

On the morning of the fifth day, we sailed through the inlet of the Chesapeake just below the tip of Cape Charles, then up the Chesapeake and on into Tangier Sound and the mouth of the Manokin River (Somerset County, Maryland).

I was amazed at the beauty of the many brick houses along the banks of this river. I later learned that houses just as beautiful lined the creeks and the rivers that flow into both sides of the Chesapeake Bay.

The captain had a friend who kept a store on the north shore of this river. He and Mr. Fitzgerald were old friends from the furniture business before the war. And so our little fleet, laden with a large bounty of gold, dropped anchor in the mouth of the Manokin River late in the afternoon as the sun was going down.

I could see his fine brick house on the shore. It had a white wooden portico in front and a broad, sloping Grecian peaked roof. The mouldings were very finely executed and there were two wings, one of wood, the other brick (the slaves' quarters). Just beyond the white picket fence which surrounded the house and yard was a long, wooden store in the Georgian style. The small panes of glass and the mouldings or mullions in the window frames are indelibly impressed upon my mind even today. The heavy deeply paneled shutters were evenly balanced, as were the panels of the doors, which were set off by heavy iron hardware. I could see all this as I stood at the bow of our ship as she lay at anchor among the other vessels.

I wanted to go ashore and see this store, but the captain assured me it was almost closing time for the proprietor usually opened at daybreak. There were always a large number of oystermen who came in early to get supplies and food before starting on their journey. We then saw the lights go out in the store, so we went down to supper and off to bed, for we were all tired.

*Gig*

# 6

*I arose early* in the morning and, without waiting for my breakfast, I took the gig—a small, round-bottomed, snub-nosed rowboat, and went ashore. I was fascinated by the beautiful brick house. I later learned that almost all the houses throughout this locality, up and down the creeks, rivers, and the shores of Chesapeake Bay, were constructed of brick manufactured in the clay hills just outside Baltimore.

As I wandered along the picket fence, I studied the lovely mouldings under the eaves and the delicately fine-carved mouldings under the portico. I looked for a long time at the window frames and their deeply recessed panel shutters. Even on Nantucket I had never seen such a fine example of Greek Revival architecture. This house was called Elmwood, and a little up the river beyond the store was another fine house called Almonington. As I looked across the river, I saw another lovely brick house, taller than the others, and I later learned that it was called Clifton. It was the ancestral home of Mrs. Fitzgerald. I proceeded along the fence, entranced by the lines and design of this lovely house.

I proceeded around the slave quarters and along the other side of the house, observing as I went that whoever painted that picket fence must have had a trying job, for one side was at least a quarter of a mile long. The entire distance around the house must have been almost a mile. As I approached the front of the house, I noticed over the door a Masonic crest with a square and G.

The help were beginning to stir in the house and smoke was curling from the chimneys. I'd always loved the smell of burning cedar wood, so I stood and drank it in. Looking down the road, I saw that the oystermen were beginning to come ashore at the store, so I dog-trotted back. The store was an oblong building, up off the ground about half a story. Apparently, the sea had once come over the lawn, for I could see water marks on the steps. As I looked back at the lovely house, I saw that it too was built half a story off the ground. The house and store stood back about two hundred feet from the river. It was apparent that the river was eating away at the bank because this small cove was directly exposed to southeast winds from across the river. It was almost equally exposed to the southwest.

I learned from our captain that the man who owned this store was a former sea captain. He had been in the East India trade, accumulated a lot of money, and then retired. He had lived in the hamlet of Baltimore, which was developing rapidly along the route of the post road from Philadelphia to the cities of the South. To get his children away from city living, he had brought his family to the eastern shore to raise them in the country. Here he had built this lovely home and store. I was equally spellbound by the store building, almost a miniature of the main house. The siding was made of matched boards and must have been put on by a ship's carpenter, for the walls were as smooth as the side of a ship. The seams between the boards could scarcely be seen and the windows were large, the panes proportioned so that they were pleasing to the eye. The mouldings of the window frames were deep and beautifully fashioned. The large shutters and their deep recessed and embossed panels were secured by magnificent black iron hardware. The shutters were painted a light grey and stood out in marked contrast to the white siding of the building. The classic design was again carried out in the roof of the store, the pitch of the slope being about ninety degrees. Beneath the peak was a fine sunburst window. The porch was covered; and the columns on the porch were square, their bases set off with fine mouldings.

I learned that Mr. Fitzgerald, the owner, supervised every piece of work which went into this building. I went up the stone steps, crossed the porch and entered the store between the double open doors. They, too, were nicely paneled, recessed and embossed. A heavy, well polished brass box lock caught my eye as I walked across the threshold. The counters were plain but carefully made and the cabinet work was superb. Beneath the glass door cabinets along the walls were closed cabinets with the same fine panels. There was a tremendous stock, particularly in the back and in the warehouse room. I wandered around, but I couldn't help but run my hand along the woodwork.

I met the owner, a charming, heavyset, kindly man, who answered all my questions, took me about, showing me much and explaining everything. As time went on, we became lasting friends.

I was standing, talking to the proprietor and asking questions about the temperature and the general climate here on the Eastern Shore of Maryland, when I turned suddenly, and there, standing in the doorway, was a beautiful young girl. She was tall and held her head high, which made her appear even statelier. She possessed an innate dignity, but her features were soft and kindly. As she stood there, she smiled pleasantly. I noticed that her complexion was fair, but slightly tanned by outdoor life. In this part of the country, the chase, the foxhunt, and riding were favorite recreations.

I saw beneath her sunbonnet that her hair was a dark brown, almost black. It was drawn slightly back from her face. Her eyes sparkled like clear spring water in the sun. Her nose was straight and on its very tip was a little flat place, which added to, rather than detracted from, her beauty. Her cheekbones were slightly prominent and a little high, but that too accentuated her loveliness. Her mouth was small, perhaps just right for the shape and size of her face. No one feature stood out but all added to the summation of her beauty.

Her shoulders were narrow. Her long flowing dress only slightly pulled in at the waist, completely disguising any suggestion of her bosom. Her hips were wide, although carefully disguised by the flowing contour of her skirt. They were just wide enough so that it wasn't necessary to wear bones or a wire frame, in the French manner, to accentuate their width. The thought which ran through my mind was that she was built just right for child bearing. I had heard my father say, "When you marry, select a girl with good shoulders, a full bosom and wide hips."

We stood there looking at each other, neither one moving. Finally her father introduced us and we seemed to talk freely from the start. I had a feeling which l cannot describe, but I remembered what the captain had told me and this was certainly it. I suggested that we go out on the porch and sit on the bench. She wanted to hear all about me and how it was up in New Jersey, for she had relatives there.

Whenever I would stop, for I wanted to hear about her, she would urge me to go on. About this time, my captain appeared on the steps of the store and remarked that I must have gotten up very early and had no breakfast — whereupon she insisted that I go over to the house and have breakfast with them. There was no arguing the point. I was interested in prolonging my visit with her and, I confess, I also wanted to see the interior of the house. So we strolled up the shore and into this fine mid-eighteenth century manor.

We entered a reception hall which extended from one side of the house to the other and I stood and gawked, as a country boy will in a strange place. There was in the hall a beautiful brass cannonball chandelier, with six candles standing in delicately curved candle stems. On the stair was a fine tall clock with a brass dial. A Palladian window graced each end of the hall. On the far side were two

*Cannonball Chandelier*

*Liquor Chest*

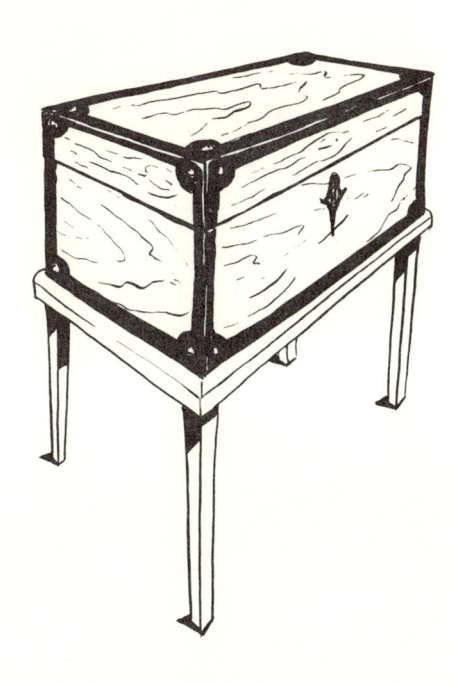

*American Girondole or Bull's Eye, after the French style. The French ones were made of plaster, the American ones were of carved wood. The French models contained candelabra, the American ones never did.*

double doors, one leading into a library, the other into a formal parlor or drawing room. The parlor was so large, it could be called a ballroom. On the floor was an East Indian rug, and between the two double doors in the hall stood a Chippendale table, flanked by two graceful Queen Anne Side chairs.

In the dining room, I gasped. I was really in love with the furnishings...but I was also in love with Helen and shamelessly I held her hand. The walls of the room were pale blue, the woodwork an oyster white. The drapes were silken, heavily lined and interlined. Their floral pattern contained a slight streak of gold thread running through the material, and the background color was gray. The dining room table was Chippendale and two hurricane globes rested at either end. A set of eight Chippendale chairs and four side chairs were arranged along the walls. Two large Sheraton windows looked out toward the river, and under each was a window bench. The sideboard was Sheraton and a French influence Bullseye convex mirror hung over the fireplace. The fireplace threw off a warm, welcome glow.

A Chinese Chippendale liquor chest stood between the windows, with fine silver handles adorning each end. Begging forgiveness, I walked over and raised the lid; there I saw twelve hand-blown bottles filled with choice liquors. Closing the lid gently, I looked across the room. On the sideboard stood two silver candelabra, each containing six candles. On the ends of the sideboard were mahogany silver-mounted knife boxes, the finest I had ever seen.

Clearly I was out of my class here. Sadness crept over me. The people who lived in this house were very wealthy. This was the kind of great wealth I had just heard about. I was a poor boy, for I hadn't made my mark in the world, and goodness knows how long this war might last. This really made me sad and I must have shown it, for Helen said, "What's wrong?"

"I should eat in the kitchen. I may smell of the sea. I really didn't expect anything like this. I'm overcome by your kindness and generosity." Again I suggested eating in the kitchen, but Helen would have none of that. She presently pulled up a chair and sat me down.

In a few moments, her mother came through the door of the dining room. She was lovely, too, extremely friendly, and carried on such a lively conversation that I was soon at ease.

In a short while, a stately old lady came through the door. She was dressed in grey and black and wore a little white bonnet trimmed with lace. She carried a long black, gold-mounted staff. At first she was haughty and not too friendly, but when she found that I came from New Jersey, and not too far from Plainfield, she broke down and welcomed me as a member of the family.

The mother sat at the foot of the table, the grandmother on the far side, next to Helen. I sat across on the other side, and presently the door opened and the head of the family entered. He sat to my right at the head of the table and asked a good old Church of England blessing, which made me feel more at home, because it was the same one we used. Then the steaming oatmeal and the homemade country sausage and griddle cakes were brought in by a little black girl by the name of Martha. She looked me over with a twinkle in her eye, turned and dashed through the door, dissolved in laughter.

I was urged and served with the utmost hospitality until I felt that if it would save me from death, I couldn't eat another thing. Then we sat back and looked across the table at each other. The grandmother, a little deaf, was beginning to make embarrassing remarks. "What are your marriage plans? When will the marriage take place? Of course it will be here." I looked at Helen. She colored slightly but smiled. The mother passed it off lightly and Mr. Fitzgerald kind of smiled, for I guess he was aware of what was going on in my heart. I was suddenly determined that nothing could deter me from making her my wife. It had happened and in a strange port.

When breakfast was over, I gave the excuse that I must return to my ship. This was a simple way to make my departure quickly and courteously, without a lot of awkward shifting.

Helen's mother suggested that Helen walk back to the ship with me. I know there was no plan beyond friendliness in her mind, and I know Captain Richard, as Mr. Fitzgerald was sometimes called, felt the same way. We departed at once and walked slowly back toward my ship. The gig was still on shore. I started to say good-bye, wishing that I had left something of importance at the house so that we might repeat the walk, but I had no such luck.

My captain was still sitting on the front porch of the store and Captain Richard had also returned. As I started to get into the gig, my captain called, "Boy, we're not sailing until late this afternoon. If you have any work to do, you can do it while we're sailing across the bay. Why don't you two young folk walk about and see some of the country?"

Helen turned to me with much enthusiasm. "Do you know how to ride?"

"Yes," I replied.

And so, with some haste, we hurried to the stable. She gave the orders to the black man and then went to the house. Soon he had saddled two horses. As I reached the front steps, Helen reappeared in an attractive green riding habit and a wide flaring pleated skirt. Her horse was brought to the block and she mounted gracefully, placing her knee over the second pommel; she rode sidesaddle. I mounted and off we went.

I had ridden broad-beamed farm horses all my life and I had ridden without saddles. I had ridden three-gaited horses, saddle horses that could plantation walk, but now that I was in a saddle and trying to ride a trotter, I soon realized that I did not know how to post. I was having the daylights pounded out of me and I know I wore a look of extreme distress, as great as that day on Long Island Sound when I lay prostrate on the deck from seasickness, although this was at the other end. Helen broke into a slow canter and my horse followed; this saved my posterior, my pride and perhaps my disposition. After that, we either walked or cantered.

I learned one thing that day. It is an easy thing to sit a trotting horse bareback with bent knees, but for some strange reason, it's practically impossible to sit a fast trotting horse comfortably under saddle without posting. I have never been able to figure out the mechanics of this.

We rode across the country that morning and, considering that I had not been on a horse for over a year and a half, I must say I did very well, for what I lacked in form, I made up in endurance. There were times we would go just about as fast as these young horses would run. As we approached houses, children would dash out to see us go flying by. These horses wanted to run; they may have sensed that they were carrying a pair of young lovers.

The morning went by quickly and all too soon we returned to the house. I was escorted upstairs by a servant to a bedroom with cardinal red drapes and carpet, comfortable chairs and a large four-poster bed. A big French tub containing warm water had been placed in front of the fireplace. I think I sat in this tub for half an hour, just dreaming what I would do if Helen promised to marry me, came north, and saw my simple home, a plain farmhouse. Supposing she was disappointed? But I passed this all out of my mind, as lovers will always do. I would live from day to day.

After my bath, I dressed and went downstairs just in time for the midday meal. I believe the main meal was eaten in the middle of the day and supper at night. I don't know whether this was the custom in this part of the South, or whether it was due to the custom of this particular family, some of whom had originally come from New Jersey.

With some embarrassment, I thanked my hostess for the second meal. But "Miss Emily" passed it off lightly. I later learned that her natural graciousness had been enhanced by her Quaker background.

We finished our meal and I said good-bye as graciously as I knew how. This time without proffered suggestion, Helen and I walked down the road to my ship. Although the road was wide, I noticed with great satisfaction that she walked close by my side. At times, even when there was no obstruction or hole in the road, she would take my arm, and when she did, I pressed her hand to my side.

My captain had said that we would leave late in the afternoon, but I had returned early. Seeing my distress at parting, he remarked, "We'd better sail now." I believe he did it to help me, but it did no good, for I did not want to leave.

In plain view of everyone, we turned and looked each other straight in the eyes. We held out our hands and, without saying a word, we knew we had to be together.

I bowed and, before releasing her hands, in a sudden impulse, I kissed them both. It seemed to come so naturally, it was without the least bit of effort or shame. I now turned and got into the gig. She gently pushed it off, and when I was a safe distance from shore, as she looked toward me and waved, I stood up and said, "I love you, Helen, as I have never loved any other girl in this whole wide world." What the captain had said just weeks before had suddenly come true.

From the look on Helen's face, I knew she knew. I called that I would be back just as soon as I could and that I would write her every day. She called back that she would do the same. As I rowed away, I realized how I had exaggerated my statement, for how could I love her more than anything else in the world when the limits of my world had been from Nantucket to Chesapeake Bay?

# 7

*We were all anxious* to impress the people on the shore and so, in real Bristol fashion, the sails went up, the fleet weighed anchor, and together with our two prizes, we set our course across the bay to Annapolis.

The wind was southwest, as it generally was that time of the year, and we sailed with a fair wind, our square-sails and tri-sails set, the main and foresail on, and the inner and outer jibs clewed down. The topsails pulled beautifully and we sailed along mostly on the quarter at about ten and one half knots.

The following afternoon, uneventfully and without speaking a ship, as the early afternoon sun was beginning to drop into the west behind the evergreen hills of Maryland, we sailed into the harbor of Annapolis. I could immediately see the beauty of this town. Most of the houses were of brick, their tall, stout chimneys built onto the end walls. Generally there were two chimneys, one at each end of the house.

As we pulled up to the dock, the doorways along the front street attracted my attention. They were mostly double, some painted red, others black or deep green, and still others a rich colonial grey. I was determined to jump ashore at the first opportunity and walk along the streets of this impressive town.

*Characteristic Annapolis roof and chimney and a close-up of Flemish Bond.*

It was the weekend and farmers were coming in with their produce. The local market was setting up and it made me homesick. I wondered what the folks were doing at home, if they had enough to eat, and whether the British were occupying our town. I was hungry for mail and as soon as we tied up, I disappeared down the companionway stairs to my bunk and wrote home, begging, as always, for news.

The mate soon called me and I knew what it meant. The men had all written their letters and they wanted me to post them at the inn, there to be picked up by the first stage going north. I bolted through the door, picked up the letters on the fly, up the stairs, across and down the deck, and up the main street as fast as I could go.

Having delivered the letters at the inn, I took a quick tour about the town. Many of the women and men were handsomely dressed, the men wearing colored weskits, silk shirts, beaver cockades. Many carried swords or sabers at their sides, and others had fine duellers stuck in at their waists beneath the sashes which held up their trousers. Their breeches were of red, grey, white or green silk or wool and their stockings were white. Their fine grain leather shoes were adorned with silver or gold buckles. Sometimes the men appeared in tall, glistening, black polished boots. These were probably men who had ridden in from the adjacent plantations.

The ladies were just as beautifully dressed in multicolored prints with typical French whale bone at the waist, which caused a marked flare of the skirt and accentuated the hips. There was much lace in evidence as they swirled along. They were accompanied either by older persons, perhaps their mothers or ladies of the household, or about three paces behind, a stout, black, woman slave.

There were all sorts of carriages, two wheel gigs with leather collapsible tops, and four wheel landaus with coachmen fore and aft, drawn by coal black or matched bay horses. Their harnesses were rich glistening brown, tan or black leather, embellished with gold or silver buckles.

There were soldiers here and there, and an occasional lagged indian. There were beautiful rich black or fiery red coaches, each drawn by fore-in hand, with a footman on the rear box or stand and one on the driver's box. The curtains were generally drawn, making it difficult to see the people inside. I saw one of these coaches at a curb and the coachman allowed me to peer in. The interior was covered with rich damask wallpaper. One coach was lined with silk, the covering of the seats in rich brocade, silk or satin.

Farm wagons of all descriptions were in evidence everywhere. Some were drawn by oxen or bullocks, some by fine, heavy horses, and others by poor hungry looking horses—the men who walked by their sides or who rode the wagons looking just as hungry. There was great wealth here and even greater poverty.

As I returned to the ship, I hoped that we might stay here for a little while. I told the captain what I had seen and he promised me that some evening he would take me up and down the streets of the town.

On the main street of the town was a charming brick inn. At a later date, the captain kept his word and took the mates and me to dinner there. Afterwards we walked up and down each of the streets of the town, observing the fine living. We later had an opportunity to see more gracious living, for the war had not struck this section. The rich, soft, mellow glow of the lamps set off the beautiful interiors against the delicate colors of the walls and woodwork.

There was fine furniture to be seen in all these homes. Some of this furniture had probably come from England a long time ago; much of it was Queen Anne. Some of it had undoubtedly been made by slaves, apprentices, master joiners and cabinet makers in that very town. These were rich experiences.

On the twelfth of December we all received letters from home. We were greatly cheered, but equally fearful because our caravan of loved ones was again on its way to spend the holiday with us. It was a long and hazardous journey across New Jersey, Pennsylvania, Delaware and Maryland.

After we had read our letters, the captain called us together and read a most interesting letter from his wife. I believe there were personal matters which he did not read, for from time to time he would pause and then begin reading again.

"Now in lonesomeness I seek the kitchen as the place where I find company, amusement suited to mirth, and games of the Negroes and the variety of visitors of the black race who frequent the place.
' I am sorry to say, Robert, that the evils of slavery continue. The white children about us are taught to tyrannize, the boy is taught to despise labor, the mind of the child is contaminated by hearing and seeing that which is not understood at the time, but remains with the memory.
"The medley of kitchen associates is increased by British soldiers who find their mess fare improved by visiting the Negroes, and by servants of officers formerly billeted in the various houses.
"All of this is very confusing perhaps to you, Robert, but such is the condition of our daily life. Many families have fled and have left this section without provision for their slaves, and so, many additional Negro families are billeted on our place.
"A regiment of British troops is stationed in our town from time to time, but just as quickly leaves.
"During the last occupation of the town by the British, I saw in my native town, particularly after the affairs of Princeton and Trenton, all the varieties and abominations of a crowded camp and garrison. An army, which had so recently passed in triumph from the sea to the banks of the Delaware, had chosen their winter quarters at their pleasure, were now driven in and crowded upon a point of land washed by the Atlantic, and defended by the guns of the ships which had borne them to the shore, as the chastisers of the rebellion.
' Here are centered, in addition to those canteened at the place, all those drawn in from the Delaware, Princeton and Brunswick, and the flower and pick of the armys, English, Scotch and German, who had at this time been brought in from Rhode Island. Here was a party of the forty-second Highlanders in national costume, and a regiment of Hessians, their dress and arms a perfect contrast to the first. The slaves of Anaspatch and Waldeck were also there. The first was somber as night; the

second, gaudy as noon. The trim and graceful English Grenadier, the careless and half-savage Highlander, with his flowing robes and naked knees, and the immovably stiff German could hardly be taken for parts of one army.

"Here might be seen soldiers driving in cattle, others guarding wagons loaded with household furniture, instead of the oats and hay for which they had been sent.

"There was the landing of the grenadiers and light infantry from the ships which transported the troops from Rhode Island, their proud march into the hostile neighborhood to gather the produce from the farmer, the sound of musketry, which soon rolled back upon us. The return of the disabled veterans who could retrace their steps, and the heavy march of the discomfitted troops, with their wagons of groaning wounded are all impressed in my mind as the picture of the evil and soul-stirring scenes of war.

"These lessons and others more disgusting, the flogging of English heroes and the thumping and caning of Germans, the brutal licentiousness, cannot help but be seen all around.

"Dear Robert, I hope and pray, that it will soon be over, and every day I hope and pray for you and the little cabin boy. We will see you soon.

"This post will reach you well before us, but we are leaving at once.

"Good-bye, my dearest."

It was evident that our dear ones were suffering. It was equally evident that the British were suffering. As soon as they advanced beyond their outposts, most particularly in small groups or at night, they were frequently pounced upon and severely mangled or destroyed. It also was equally evident that they had found it too costly to hold Amboy.

# 8

*I was receiving* letters regularly from my own dear one across the bay on the eastern shore. I answered them immediately when possible, and posted them at the inn. The letters I received told me what my dear Helen was doing, but they were a little on the formal side. In my letters, however, I poured out my heart and my love. I knew that I must see her. I must find out what my chances were to make her my wife. I longed to be at her side. Every minute of that evening and the following morning I had spent with her were indelibly impressed upon my mind, and I lived them over and over a hundred times.

At a meeting of the fleet officers, our captain distinguished himself not only by his eloquence, but by the character of his reasoning. He told the captains and mates that the best thing for us all to do was scatter. As rapidly as prizes were taken, the worthwhile salable materials could be sold at Annapolis, the money taken to the head of the *Elk* and placed in the custody of the small garrison there, then on to Robert Morris by a rapid wagon march. The officers were in agreement, and so the following day the fleet broke up, but we remained at Annapolis for refitting.

On the eighteenth of December, according to the records in my diary, I attended a session of the Colonial Legislature at Annapolis, where I heard the brilliant Mr. Carroll plead, extoll, coerce, and threaten the opposition, until finally the members of the legislature, almost to the man, backed him and decided that there would definitely be no reunion with the Crown. I was also happy to hear that Maryland would send another regiment to General Washington. The talk in the coffee houses, the inn, the churches, in street gatherings, and at the slave market was now of independence.

Frontiersmen were coming in from the west of Maryland and joining up. One day they looked like a ragged lot; the next day they were dressed in the beautiful green Maryland uniforms, drilling, and looking better each day. In a few days they were marching northward to join our general.

I recall that when Mr. Carroll described the transactions of the last convention in Philadelphia to the State Legislature, or more properly, the State Committee of Safety, he waxed warm and heated when he mentioned John Adams. It seems that the news came in of the British defeat at Red Bank on the Delaware and the death of Dunop (the Hession general who was in command at Trenton on that eventful Christmas night). The British had lost the Augusta and Merlen, two great frigates; as they floated down the Delaware River they grounded and the next day they were set afire by hot shot from the American galleys and floating batteries, and blown up before all of their crew could escape. We recovered two twenty-four-pounders. At this point, Mr. Carroll said, John Adams jumped up and cried aloud, "Thank God glory is not immediately due to the commander in chief, or idolatry or adulation would have been so excessive as to endanger our liberties!"

Several weeks later, Carroll was still as hot and fiery as the color of his hair. How could anyone accuse our great general of even an inclination or thought of becoming a monarch. He had stated his position so clearly on so many occasions that when I went home and told our captain of this incident, he wagged his head.

"Yes," he said, "there are many who would destroy this great man for their own selfish ends. I see them every day in this town. They come to the dock in their finery and with their snuff boxes wanting to know when we'll bring in prizes. The thought of personal gain, in a war in which our great army is suffering all sorts of privations, nauseates me.

"Certainly these people can pay for this finery. They're selling the produce of their farms, horses, meats, food and fuel, and getting hard cash for it. They're paying no taxes and there is no organization of the privateersmen. How could we hope that our great general would obtain all the money he needs so much. If the money from our captured ships had been turned over to Robert Morris, there would have been no necessity for him to beg from door to door for help.

' It won't be so easy to take these ships from now on. Word has now gotten back to England, and all of the great ships will now be heavily armed units of the King's Navy. Our only hope to help is to attack the coastwise Loyalists' ships.

' It will be necessary for us to be on the alert night and day. Repeat nothing to anyone, no matter how friendly he may seem, and keep a careful record of any successes we may have and any moneys we may take. The Continental Congress here is loyal, but it lacks experience. It is legislative, like all the colonial legislatures, but its judiciary is weak. This is a good place from which to sail and sell captured material, for the people have money. And there are ever so many creeks, inlets and rivers in which we can hide. Between Mr. Pearsall and myself, we know them all.'

# 9

*On the twenty-fourth* of December, 1777, the caravan arrived with our loved ones from home. It was not to be a very happy Christmas for me, because I didn't even have enough money with which to buy a gift for my relatives or my beloved, for that matter. What little pleasure I had during this holiday, I did so by attending the legislature, where I heard the latest news brought by couriers.

When our caravan arrived, it pulled directly to the public dock. Their trip had been long and arduous. It had been necessary to bypass Philadelphia, for the British were there and the back roads were in poor condition from repeated snow, sleet and ice. This trip had been a real hardship. It showed most particularly on the women.

The slaves had been left at home to take care of the farms. The responsibility for holding back the British was falling upon the small garrisons in the towns and upon Captain Edgar's troop of light horse which seemed to be everywhere.

When Howe went into winter quarters at Philadelphia and Clinton to his in New York, they ordered the garrison at Amboy to withdraw across Staten Island and on back to New York. The only opposition left was from the Loyalists, who occupied some stretches of Staten Island, and a garrison under Knypenhausen at St. George.

After Major Simcoe's disastrous foray around New Brunswick and the town of Blazing Star, and after their two defeats at Lyons Farm and Springfield, where they were compelled to retreat down Morris Avenue and through Elizabeth to Staten Island, never again did a British soldier set foot on New Jersey soil. When the general campaign was transferred to the south into Virginia, the Carolinas and the Georgia plantations, the New Jersey people felt relief for the first time since the war had begun.

Militarily, this transfer of campaign was one of the greatest mistakes of the war, for the iron furnaces along the Mullica River were turning out shot, the farms throughout the entire colony of New Jersey were turning out produce, and supplying beef cattle, horses, and clothing. The charcoal furnaces in the southeastern part of the state were producing shot, cannon ball, and charcoal for gunpowder in enormous quantities. The women in the churches and meeting houses were making clothing and uniforms. The busy gunsmiths and forgers were repairing arms which had been gathered up from time to time by boys on the battlefields after battles, for which they obtained ten cents for each gun, bayonet and cartridge box. These were then transported by wagon loads to the local gunsmiths.

The tragedies which befell our families, most particularly the families in and around Amboy during the British occupation, were appalling. Their homes were literally destroyed, their silverware and furniture stolen by the troops going back to England. More than just occasionally, young girls were raped in their homes and mothers were raped in the presence of their children. The casual way in which the British officers dismissed these frightful atrocities showed in the drawn and sorrowful faces of our dear ones.[10]

The last meeting of the Maryland Legislature was in session before the Christmas holidays. As we walked to the door, the red and green coated liveried Negroes at the door whispered and placed their fingers to their lips for silence. As we sat down in the gallery, Mr. Carroll was on his feet.

"Ladies and Gentlemen, with Burgoyne's surrender, it became the paramount duty of Gates to detach reinforcements to Washington, but weeks have passed and even the corps of Maryland has not arrived. Therefore, our commander in chief, at the end of October, dispatched his noble aide, Alexander Hamilton, with the authority to demand them. This was followed by the strangest incidents. For a while Putnam disregarded orders borne by Hamilton. Gates, in his elation, detained a large part of his army in idleness at Albany under the pretext of an expedition to Ticonderoga, which he did not mean to attack and which the British themselves abandoned. He neglected to announce his victory to the commander in chief and sent the tardy message directly to Congress: 'With an army in health, vigor and spirits, Major General Gates now awaits the command of the honorable Congress.'

"Think of it, my friends, passing by our beloved general! Instead of chiding the insubordination, Congress appointed him to regain the forts and passes on the Hudson River. Now Washington had himself recovered these forts and passes by pressing Howe so closely as to compel him to order their evacuation. Yet Congress forbade Washington to detach from the northern army more than 2500 men, including the corps of Morgan, without first consulting General Gates and the governor of New York.

"It was even moved that he should not detach any troops, except after consultation with Gates, Clinton, Samuel Adams, John Adams and Geary of Massachusetts. Oh yes, Marchond of Rhode Island also voted for that restriction.

"Time was wasted by this interference. And while the northern army had been borne onward to victory, with the rising of the people in Pennsylvania, Washington encountered disaffection and internal friction. Thus the opportunity of driving Howe from Philadelphia before the winter was lost. I ask you, would any other general stand for this nonsense? I see by your faces, by the nods of your heads, that you agree unequivocally—No! How much offense should a man of this caliber be required to stand? I ask you to decide by vote. I ask this legislature to go on record, and to write it into the minutes, that we send to Philadelphia a vote of complete confidence in our commander in chief, and that he be the commander in chief not only in name but in deed."

As Mr. Carroll sat down, a corpulent individual arose and made the motion. He was rapidly followed by a wizened little fellow, who seconded the motion. A vote was quickly cast and the motion passed unanimously.

I thought, as I sat there, of the loyalty of the black people, whom the various agents of the King had tried to incense against the whites, and how they stood loyally by us. I made up my mind that the first person in the future who ever talked about religion and color in an unkindly way would draw my fire at once.*

If the British had remained in control of Amboy and had forced the patriots out, or subjected them to continuous military occupation, I learned that the captain had planned to move all of our people down and settle them in a suitable place on the eastern shore of Maryland. Next to home, I believe he loved this place more than any other in the world. However, this had become unnecessary, for just as soon as the British sent troops out in any direction from New York or into New Jersey, they were severely mauled and their equipment destroyed. Even within their own camp, their equipment was damaged and the food sold to them was frequently spoiled or tainted. They lived in constant fear of being poisoned.

Therefore, the British were glad to get away from such a hot bed as New Jersey, just as they had been glad to get out of New England earlier. The captain was again very restless and anxious to get our people started home, particularly since the King's army had withdrawn from New Jersey.

At dinner in the inn on Christmas Day, he openly stated that when one sees his loved ones, it doesn't make much difference how long they stay, just so long as they are seen. Therefore, fearful of the weather after the first of the year, he insisted that the families depart the day after Christmas.

---
*Carroll of Carrollton was Catholic.

The rest of Christmas Day, the ladies busied themselves repairing our uniforms, sewing on buttons, and generally improving our appearance. They presented us with our new flag, the American (Betsy Ross) flag. As our captain accepted the new flag, he laughingly said, "Presenting flags to us, by you ladies, is becoming a custom."

That night the married men slept in the inn and I slept aboard ship in my bunk, almost completely at peace with myself and happy in all my thoughts—except that I missed my dear Helen. I remembered what our captain had said. "Never cross a bridge until you come to it, but when you come to it, never fail to cross it." A great change was coming over me. I was too young to know what that change was, but I no longer had the usual desires. I was planning my future and my home, and with happy thoughts of Helen, I fell asleep.

# 10

*On the twenty-seventh* of December, 1777, we fell down the bay from Annapolis, through Tangier Sound, and up into the mouth of the Manokin River. I thought at first that the captain had done this for me, but I soon realized we had come over here to fit out and provision, because both were much cheaper to do on this shore. There were good ship fitters and riggers at a dollar a day, all the way from Deal's Island up to the head of the Manokin.

My heart beat wildly when I realized that I was soon to be near my dear Helen, but I was soon depressed, for I recalled that I did not have so much as a handkerchief for her. It was almost dark when we dropped anchor. I could see the lights go out in the store and the lights go on in the big manor house.

In deep thought, I ate my supper slowly, and pushed the food around on the plate with my fork. The men were discussing politics and wondering how their families were getting along on their long trek home. They were discussing the strategy of the unfolding plan of the British with their new campaign in the South. I recall hearing the captain comment that we were going on down to Yorktown and make a direct report to the Continental Congress. He would try to find out if all the money we had sent had arrived. I heard these remarks but otherwise caught only fleeting wisps of the conversations.

Finally the captain tapped me on the shoulder and beckoned me to come along with him. I followed him into his quarters and he began to pile boxes on the table. Then he began to separate them. He looked at me, smiled, then patted me on the shoulder and put his arm about me in the most fatherly manner. Finally, when three packages had been placed at one end of the table, he told me they were my gifts for Helen. He carefully and meticulously unwrapped them; there were laces and multicolored silks and woolens, linens and cottons. I gasped and he was pleased.

"You know, Alexander, I know something about this young lady that you do not. She is an excellent dressmaker and dresses in the latest fashions because she watches the sketches and prints as they appear in the yearbook from Paris." The third box contained a beautiful sweeping bonnet with wide ribbon streamers. As I held it up, I could almost see Helen's lovely head beneath it.

The captain carefully rewrapped them and as I went off to bed, I wondered if he had really come over here to fit and repair and provision because it was cheaper, or did he actually come over to deliver these presents to his friends? I wondered.

I was awake with the first cock crow at the rays of dawn. I dressed hurriedly, went on deck, and looked off toward the shoreline. All was quiet except for smoke coming from the chimney of the slave kitchen. How could I ever wait until the proper hour for a gentleman to call? What time would the proper hour be? Most certainly it couldn't be before ten in the morning. And so, in order that I might be visible from the big house, I decided to climb about the ship and do all sorts of silly things in an attempt to appear busy and be seen. As the day came on, people began to move toward the store and about the yard of the main house. Some began to feed the stock and boatmen began to gather, awaiting the opening of the store. Finally, as I heard the windows of the great house close, I couldn't help but straighten up and look directly toward it; but the windows were being closed by slaves and there was no sign of the one I loved.

*116*

Our crew was beginning to assemble for breakfast, so I went below and, I must admit, ate a very hearty meal. I was beginning to take a little ribbing from all except dear old Richard. Breakfast finally over, as much to get away from the ribbing as to see my dear one, I ascended the companionway steps and looked across the deck toward the house. There standing on the great front porch, catching my eye at the moment mine caught hers, was Helen.

She was waving wildly. I raised my cockade and waved wildly in reply, my enthusiasm unbounded. Leaping to the side rail and out on the stays, I almost went overboard, for I forgot "one hand for the ship and one hand for yourself" and let loose my other hand. She started down the steps of the great house as I disappeared down the companionway steps. Before I could ask the captain, he nodded his head and said, "Yes, boy, go and enjoy yourself. Now is the time to do your courting, while we are fitting out and provisioning, for there will be nothing for you to do. Take the gig and packages, and be gone with you."

I have no words to describe the speed with which I took to the gig, armed with my gifts, and rowed ashore. As the boat struck bottom, I jumped into the water and splashed ashore. With outstretched arms, meaning to take her by the hand, I found that she was in my arms. My surprise was so great that tears were in my eyes. We swung along to the house and there she spread her presents upon the elegant Chippendale dining room table. In that charming setting, they looked even more beautiful. When she reached the hat box, uncovered it and placed the bonnet upon her head, I stood in awe. Finally she came to my side, took me in her arms and embraced me. At that moment her mother walked in, but as quickly retired. It was the greatest Christmas I have ever had. I never forgot it.

Helen draped the pieces of material at her side or around her shoulders. I realized how beautiful they would look when made up into dresses and in these lovely surroundings. Her father walked in and greeted me warmly. He was then followed by her mother, who acted as though she'd seen nothing. I was to spend a long, pleasant holiday with them.

We visited her friends in the countryside and rode over to the small towns, villages and hamlets. We rode over to Mount Vernon wharf and visited other nearby country stores. One warm early January day we rode all the way down to Deal's Island, where we saw dugout canoes built by the Indians. They would fell trees in the forest, using a straight log for the keel and slightly curved logs for the sides, and fasten them together with wooden pegs. Then they would burn and chop out the interior and exteriors, and smoothe the surfaces. They made fine, graceful log canoes.

We rode to the lovely town of Princess Anne and met many of Helen's friends. We visited the Teagle Mansion and went through this beautiful late eighteenth century home. It had a wide and high central hall. The two side wings were plain and were held to the center by colonnades; the mansion had great dignity. We had lunch at the old hotel, which was a coach stop for the Eastern Shore. We rode about the town and enjoyed visiting with everyone we met. Then we rode home.

We attended several dances and holiday parties during my stay. I found the people, both Helen's relatives and her friends, equally hospitable. They were very kind, very friendly, and—I say with due modesty—proud of what the *Blazing Star* had done. In fair weather we rode great distances on young horses. This kept me trim and hardened me, and I learned to post. In bad weather we either sat about the store, or actually waited on customers. Other times we sat and talked in the great house by the fire and, I confess, caressed more than a little.

The day before the third of January, the day on which we were to depart for Yorktown, I asked Helen if I might seek her father's permission for her hand in marriage. She said yes and I was thrilled. I dashed to the store and, gathering up all my courage, with a deep breath I burst into the store—and there my power of speech left me. I

Log Canoe

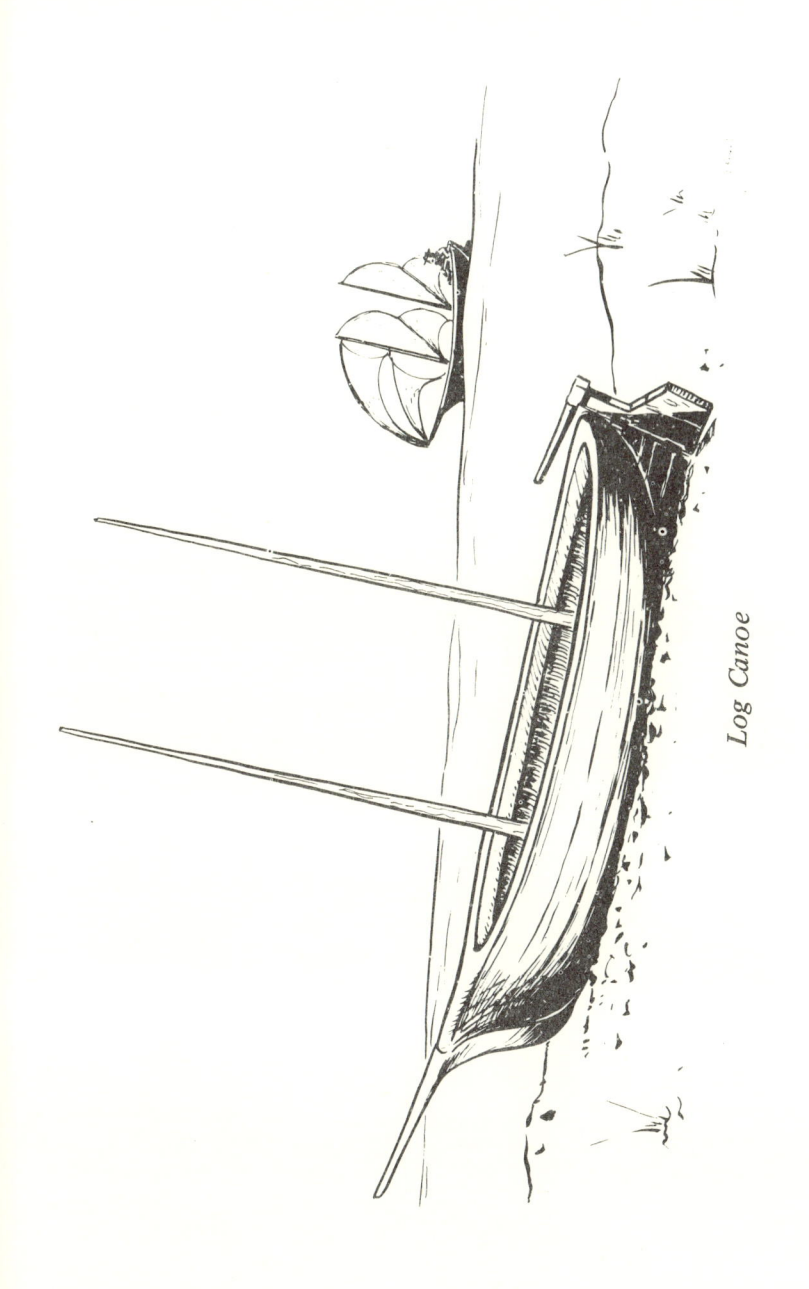

shifted from one foot to the other. I ran my hand up and down the counter. Mr. Fitzgerald, who was alone in the store, came up to me and said kindly, "What's the matter, my son? Can I help you?"

With that, my courage returned and I burst out, "Mr. Fitzgerald, may I have permission to marry your daughter?"

"Why, yes," he said, then patted me on the back and continued with a smile. "Nothing would make me happier. I was about to close the store anyway. Let's close up and go back to the house and have some dinner."

We walked back together. He was so kind and friendly that he made it much easier for me as we entered the great house. I don't believe I ever did ask Mrs. Fitzgerald for her daughter's hand. I always meant to, but I guess she felt that in asking the skipper's permission I had suffered enough.

After a fine dinner we all sat around and talked, and at about nine o'clock the folks went off to bed. Helen and I sat in front of the fire. There was no further mention of the past now; we were planning for the future. Helen said she thought the engagement should last at least a year, for in that time we would both be very sure.

Finally, as the coals in the fire began to flicker and die, we closed the iron doors which held the heat and said good night with a long embrace. After that I was sure that Helen loved me. I promised to see her early in the morning before sailing and I returned to my ship with a light heart.

This was not to be, however, for we sailed at daybreak with the tide, dropping down the river into Tangier Sound, and on down into the bay. With a strong northwest wind, we sailed on to new adventures and Yorktown.

# 11

*Yorktown became* the colonial capital of the thirteen colonies and the Continental Congress, driven out of Philadelphia by the arrival of Howe. They could not have selected a more desirable place for their own safety. It would take an enormous fleet to surround the peninsula between the York and James rivers. It would also take a fabulous army, marching down the peninsula, to surround it from the land side. Escape was afforded up the peninsula by a series of good roads, or by ferry across a number of small rivers and the much larger York, Rappahannoc and James. Thus the Congress could retire out of reach of a British army in a few hours and in almost any direction.

These facts must have influenced Cornwallis at a later date in selecting this point as a basis for operation, for without the French blockade, he would have been safe there. And without the French army, things might have been different on the land side, but that is another story.

Our sail down the bay was uneventful, except that we met and passed many ships whose loyalty was uncertain. We later learned that most of these were coastwise vessels, more interested in making money than helping our righteous cause. They were not only carrying supplies for the British, but were actually serving as spies, for gold.

The days were getting longer, but the weather was still cold and few days were clear. Still we made the 70 miles to Yorktown in one day and before dark. We lay at anchor off the town dock at the mouth of the York River; this was a busy port. Both sides of the town dock were lined with ships, and many other ships were lashed to them, lying side by side.

There were a great many privateers here and a great many prizes; business had been good. We all hoped that the Continental Congress was receiving the money from these prizes and receiving it all. To be out of the way, we moved our anchorage to a little sheltered cove at the mouth of a small fresh water stream behind Yorktown on the northwesterly side. In so doing, the barnacles would fall off the ship's hull. Here we threw out our anchor, put everything in order, and went down for supper.

I ate as though I were in a trance. Many times I was spoken to, but scarcely heard, and rarely did I answer. On more than one occasion I heard members of the crew say, "The boy can't help it. He's in love."

Yes, I was in love, and I was disturbed because I had been unable to see Helen in the morning. I knew it would be a great disappointment for her to find that we had sailed. I was determined to write her now and post it as early as I could in the morning.

That night the captain and the men sat about the cabin before a brisk fire. I retired to my bunk, but I couldn't sleep. I lay awake for hours, tossing from side to side. All the things Helen and I had done together returned to my mind. I could recall every little detail of the hours and the days we had spent together. I got up, lit the candle, and reread the letter I had written, but there was nothing more I could say, so I sealed it with wax and went back to bed. Finally I fell asleep.

I was awakened in the morning by one of the sailors, for I had overslept, and there was much work to be done. We had not completed the minor details of our fitting out. We were in a strange port and we wanted to look our very best, so we busied ourselves throughout the day, preparing our ship for a possible inspection by the Continental Congress. This never came, but our size, our trimness, and our reputation caused the captains of many of the privateers to come aboard. They made notes of many items and sometimes remarked that they were going to apply this or that to their own ship. They all remarked about how small we really were.

During the day the captain appeared before the Continental Congress. After going through a great pile of receipts and records, he found that not all the money he had collected had been turned in or accounted for. While waiting, I leaned over the taff rail and looked toward the land, but there was little I could see, for the town was on the other side of the hill. But the countryside was beautiful. Off in the distance on either shore of the river I could see farm houses of both wood and brick. They appeared to be a story and a half high, oblong in shape and simple in structure, with stoops instead of porches, frequently with dormers cut through the steep roof, and huge chimneys at either end, an American version of Elizabethan. I was burning to get ashore.

As the afternoon wore on, the news spread from ship to ship that we were in port. Late in the afternoon a captain came aboard. I showed him to the captain's quarters and there learned it was Captain John Trumble from Connecticut. He had been in port at Sagg Harbor with us, and he brought us a very important message. It seems that the royal governor of New Jersey, Governor Franklin, having been transported to Connecticut for safe keeping, had gotten word to General Clinton in New York about the exploits of our little vessel. Clinton had instructed his adjutant general to search out a ship builder on Staten Island who was loyal to the King and have him construct a schooner which he could guarantee would be as fast and as maneuverable as our little schooner. She was to search us out and take us, if possible; if not, she was to destroy us. And so, on the far side of Staten Island at St. George, such

*A Typical Tidewater Virginia house—large chimneys, often set back as they rise, steep Elizabethan roofs. Simplicity of design, nice doorways, and stoops instead of porches.*

a schooner had been constructed, of 83 foot water line with a superior stern armament. Three guns pointed out the stern or transom windows, at least twelve guns, six on a side, on the deck, and two guns swiveled off the bow. She was built for speed and maneuverability, and therefore could be easily identified by her long bow sprite and long main boom. I was frightened, but Captain Hunter sat there without so much as a change in his expression, smoked his churchwarden pipe, and whatever he thought, he didn't even confide in Captain Trumble.

Captain Trumble did say that the small privateersmen now intended to work on coastwise shipping in small groups. They all had a description of this schooner and, although they did not know her name, they intended to destroy her on sight. The last time she was seen, she was reported by a coastwise merchantman, supposed to be in Clinton's service, actually one of our men and a spy. He had seen her cruising off Little Egg, but no one had seen her since. That was in the middle of November.

Prizes were coming in daily. They ranged all the way from small sloops, scarcely more than bay or river sloops, to brigs and barks, and even slow, clumsy, square riggers, some of them of ancient vintage with rigging so old that I had never seen that type of sail before. Some were schooners, but they were not graceful schooners. They were very full in the wrong places—like an ugly woman.

I never did see the Congress in session, but I stood outside the door and had various people pointed out to me as they went through. I recognized Mr. Carroll as he walked through, Mr. Randolph from Virginia, and Samuel P. Chase from Maryland.

Yorktown is a very small hamlet. I expected to find a larger town, perhaps because I now compared everything to Annapolis. There was no grandeur about the houses. The shutters were plain and the hardware often ill-fashioned. The doorways were not smart and elegant like those on the great homes of the Eastern Shore. The streets were of dirt and there was nothing very charming about the local people. The girls were not comely or pretty; the men were not handsome. The town appeared to be a shipping port of lesser importance and there was certainly no sign of great wealth, except among some members of Congress whose possessions were on a par with those seen at Annapolis.

I don't know what the interior of the great colony of Virginia was like, for I never saw it. I have heard that there are many beautiful mansions and plantations, but this seaport section gave me the impression of a run-down, threadbare area. None of it could compare with the grandeur of Maryland, Sagg Harbor, or Little Egg at its best.

Except for the fleet of privateersmen and the Continental Congress, this section was most certainly drab. If it had ever had a greatness, it was all gone now, for even the houses were illkept, many in need of paint and repair. The people appeared to be indifferent and inclined to keep to themselves, yet they were friendly enough when approached. It may have been that they had seen much poverty. They seemed to be so many miles from nowhere. There wasn't a single girl in the town who could be compared to my dear one, although the girls and the women seemed very respectable. It looked like progress had moved on and the people who'd guessed wrong remained behind.

The weather was becoming dirtier every day. The fogs were increasing in frequency and snow flurries were occurring at regular intervals. The wind constantly blew out of the northeast and when it did shift, it blew straight down from the north or northwest. The thermometer fell each day. We were completely immobilized and burned so much wood that it was necessary to replenish our supply on three different occasions. There we were, down at the mouth of the York River in the shadows of the fugitive colonial capital, with nothing to do but sit and wait for spring. Fortunately the capital was nearby and couriers on horseback traversed this bitter weather. Wagons, stagecoaches and carriages took mail through to the home colonies. In that way our mail was taken out and we occasionally heard from home.

# 12

*One morning,* sometime after the fifteenth of March, a new man came aboard. He presented himself to the captain as Edward Cook. He had walked all the way down from Monmouth, New Jersey. He said he lived along the north shore of the Manasquan River. Having heard of our fame and the good things we were doing from the watermen along Barnegat Bay, he wanted to join up. When the captain asked him what he could do, he replied with a ready smile, "I guess I ain't much of a sailor, but I'm a good boatman and a fair shot with a longarm." He was short and stocky, and seemed to be about 55 or 60 years of age. When the captain offered him a twist, he touched his hat respectfully and took it. He claimed he could hit a silver dollar at one hundred yards and, smiling, added, "If I had one." But he said he hadn't seen a silver dollar in so long, he wasn't sure he would know one if he saw it. The captain signed him on at once. He was just the kind of fellow we needed to liven up the sometimes depressing days.

Within the next few days two frigates came in, one captained by Isaac Hull, the other by Ira Hand. They had come from down along Salem way in New Jersey. When the captain saw these two frigates drop anchor and learned who their commanders were, he called the men together.

"Men, this is our opportunity to learn the use of hot-shot. These are the two men who can teach us. They're masters!" And so, with Mr. Sykes, Mr. Pearsall, and two sailors, the captain put out in the gig, first to the one frigate and then the other. They were gone for half a day, and when they came back, they had the information they had been seeking. Their enthusiasm was now unbounded.

That afternoon we all gathered in the captain's quarters. "Mr. Cook," said the captain, "I sometimes think you were God sent, for with you we now have a working group which I believe is unbeatable. You will vie with the boy in your marksmanship. You will be the official sharpshooter. Your position will be the foretop and, son, yours will remain the maintop, for you are accustomed to that position and have done well. Meanwhile we will sail up the river, fire into the sand dunes and dig out the shot. We will practice the use of hot-shot slowly at the start and try to increase our efficiency. I will leave it to you, Mr. Cook, and to you, my boy, to practice your marksmanship." And so Mr. Cook and I went ashore in the gig and practiced shooting cattails at one hundred yards.

I would like to say that I finally became as proficient as Mr. Cook, but that would not be the truth. But he was my inspiration and taught me a great deal, and I improved my marksmanship to the satisfaction of the captain. The men practiced with hot-shot, wheeling the guns back and forth across the deck. We were still using charcoal in the pots because the fires could be lighted and blown up without being seen at any distance, and charcoal is very hot. This was essential to hot-shot.

There were times when members of Congress appeared on the hill to watch us. This was an incentive for other privateers, for soon many of them were doing the same. But most of them were so anxious to bring in prizes that each time they returned immediately to the sea. We had other plans. We had a special ship to meet, a heavier armed ship, a larger ship, probably manned by men of the regular service, a ship sent out to destroy us.

*Fire rail with powder trench*

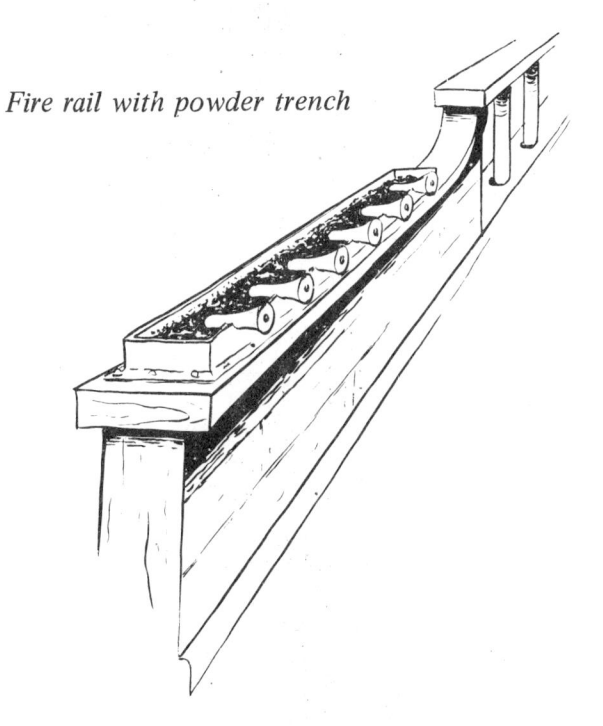

*Enlargement of the touch hole in the end of a short blunderbuss*

*Chain Shot*

*The brick floor over the deck and its pot*

*Ladle for carrying hot shot*

We practiced quick handling of our ship trying to increase our efficiency in going about, for I could see the captain's ambition was now to meet and take the *King's Mistress*, as we were now calling our mystery rival. We still did not know her true name. From time to time, we shifted our powder and other stores in the hold to improve our efficiency in sailing. We tested our speeds under various positions of the cargo, and when we had determined the best fore and aft position, Mr. Springer made a level to fit midships on the deck so that we could constantly maintain our best position under sail and keep our ship trim.

Finally, satisfied that no more improvements could be made, on the first of April, fully provisioned and with the entire crew in the best of health, we set sail from Yorktown, out the inlet, around Cape Charles and up the coast, to accept the challenge.

We met several privateers coming in with prizes — wretched prizes. They were now reduced to taking anything across the board. Some of these ships were miserable looking arks, but I daresay that many of them had important cargos.

We sailed up along the coast of Maryland and I was very sad because day by day I was moving farther away from my dear Helen. Would I ever live to return? Why should we accept the challenge of the *King's Mistress*. Yet we must, for it was a matter of honor now.

Our ship was running without lights, for we were all alone, approaching the mouth of the Delaware. Here we might encounter great ships, ships going to Philadelphia and the British army, even troopships and frigates. We gave the Delaware a wide berth and proceeded up the coast of New Jersey. The ocean was cold, but the weather was warm. The sun was regaining a good deal of its power, the days were clear and the winds were south. We were kiting along before the wind, all sails set.

We flew our new flag now, the American flag, the flag of the thirteen colonies with its thirteen brilliant white stars circled on a field of blue. What a beautiful flag it was! We had a wonderful crew, which got along fine together. Mr.

Cook was always jolly and happy, always telling stories, some funny, some serious. He liked to tell stories of ladies of the evening, but he always told them in such a manner that no one could ever take offense.

We didn't see a single ship from the time we came up past the Delaware until we hailed Little Egg Inlet. As we sailed through the inlet, we recognized a number of our old friends again riding in Little Egg Bay. When we sailed through the lines, the men waved, and occasionally a pistol shot was fired. But as for the town, I couldn't believe my eyes!

As we sailed on up to the one little dock, I realized what a different town it was. There were no longer any factories and it was evident that it would never occupy its former glory. Five houses remained and they were only shacks. After we had tied up and gone ashore, we were told that the people had been so discouraged by the hurricane and the British attack that they had moved inland some 20 miles and had established a new town. But as we looked across and up toward Tuckertown, there was evidence that new homes were rising there and all along the upper bay; the courage of the people had returned. They were building new homes and settling down to a new form of life.

The few houses at Little Egg were near the dock, and prize materials were being unloaded. There were two prize ships at the dock and several of the captains immediately came aboard. They told our captain that from time to time this new British schooner, manned by Loyalists, had been spotted off the mouth of the Delaware even as far south as Cape Charles. Her general rendezvous was kept somewhere between New York and Little Egg. Many of them had had a close call with her on more than one occasion and some of their crew members had been killed. Sometimes only nightfall, fog or snow had saved them from capture and death on the *Jersey,* for that infamous prison ship was still behind Sandy Hook Island, loaded with miserable, wretched prisoners. When the wind was onshore, the stench from the sick, the dying and the filth could be smelled for miles.

I noticed that the captain narrowed his eyes, clenched his fist and automatically placed his right hand on his pistol, but he said nothing. Then they all sat down to a glass of Madeira and talked about the major campaign which had shifted to the South. The South was now suffering and all agreed that something should be done to give them relief. A fleet of frigates should be built and sent to the relief of Charleston and Gifford's Inlet. Clinton had been immobilized in New York by Washington all winter and his army had also suffered for want of fresh food, but unfortunately the New York civilian population had suffered even more. What there was, Clinton took.

After the others had left, our captain called all the men together. He repeated all the news he had heard and instructed us all to write letters home, but to tell our families to be sure to burn them and not to talk, for there were still plenty of Loyalists and Tories and dangerous Quakers near their homes. We would lie in port for at least a week with the hope of attracting the *King's Mistress* to the mouth of Little Egg, for there were many false mouths here to pass along the news that we were in.

We went far up into the creek where we couldn't be seen and we practiced daily with hot-shot,[1][2] and when it hit the banks at low tide, it squirmed, hissed and jumped about like an injured serpent. Having heard stories from the several captains as to the strength and formidableness of our adversary, I was quite frightened. Why wouldn't it be just as clever to dodge such a formidable adversary? Why look for trouble? I slept poorly at night, and when I did, I thrashed about, dreaming I was fighting from the maintop. I would awaken from a sound sleep with the feeling of warm blood dripping down my body, but it was only warm sweat. Then I would think of the beautiful peace and quiet of the eastern shore and my Helen, and I doubted I would ever see her again. Many men had been killed trying to fight this schooner; some of these ships were armed as well, if not better, than we. Several of our privateersmen had been taken and our men cruelly treated. However, if any of the other men were frightened, they didn't show it.

# 13

*On the first day* of May, 1778, a small bark came into the inlet. The men were frantically waving over the bow. She sailed right up through the fleet, went about close enough to our little schooner to hail us and give us the news. The *King's Mistress* was less than five miles off Little Egg Inlet and "asailing" back and forth. The challenge had come!

The chills moved up and down my spine, down to my knees and on to the bottoms of my feet. My knees buckled and it became necessary for me to hold the fife rail or I'm sure I would have fallen. I looked about at the men. With the exception of the captain, Mr. Sykes, Mr. Pearsall and Mr. Springer, I thought the men looked frightened, but I wasn't sure. On second thought, I don't think Mr. Cook looked very frightened. He patted the butt of his long tom rifle and a cheerful smile spread across his ruddy countenance. "Here we go, boy," he said, and immediately went forward to his station at the foot of the foremast and placed his hand on the braces. He was ready! I dashed down for my rifle and went to my station. While I was gone, the men had already run up the sails. They were hauling in the anchor and we were now underway.

I was too young to die. Suppose I lived and had an arm or leg blown off? There were lots of people moving around Little Egg this way. Would Helen still marry me?

*The King's Mistress*

I had little feeling of a sense of duty now. Given the slightest excuse, I believe I would have gone ashore. My teeth chattered. The captain saw it and called me to the poop deck. "My boy, I want you to have confidence in me and I want you to have confidence in yourself. You can't do a good job today unless you have confidence in me and yourself. You must make every charge of your musket count. A great deal will depend on you and Mr. Cook, for we're counting on you to pick the men away from the guns. We cannot refuse this challenge; you know that. If you have to die, die gloriously. In the past, others have done as much for you." Then he turned from me and addressed the men:

"Men, have no fear, if you do as you have in the past, we will write a worthy page in American history today. Although we may fight a worthy adversary from the standpoint of armament, I don't believe they can equal us in ability as marksmen. I don't believe their ship will be able to take any more than ours will, for if she's fast, she must have been built light. Remember, our planking is of straight grained oak, and our ribs of locust. Our knees are of the heart of hackberry and the forged iron of our good ship's supporting parts was made by one of the finest blacksmiths in New Jersey.* Never despair for a moment!" He then thanked the men and they all returned to their stations.

In the two weeks preceding this eventful day we had constructed a cedar raft and placed upon it a small mast, with a sail and two kegs. One contained fresh water and the other hard biscuits cooked by Richard.

We had been instructed that if our adversary went down and our ship went down also, we would float this raft off the poop deck and the survivors could sail for shore. If we went down and they did not, only God could help us! This was the situation as we emerged from Little Egg Inlet on the first day of May in 1778.

---

*Dave Gilman

*131*

Every man was at his station. Each wore a brace of pistols in his sash, a tomahawk* and a sailor's knife. Every man had a loaded musket at his side and extra loaded muskets were placed along the fife rail. A fire rail was also set up. The men were looking eagerly over the side now, toward the horizon. Some were chewing tobacco, some their pipe stems. Straight out ahead, not more than five miles, stood the schooner.

Our mates were studying her through their glasses and all of us were appraising her, protecting our eyes with our hands. As we looked at her, she didn't appear any larger than we were. She was going about now, heading directly toward us and the inlet. The wind was steady and strong, coming directly out of the south, as it usually does about the first of May. The seas were even and small, but contained a little whiteness to their caps. We rose and fell gently and, I thought, proudly. The fire was now struck in the pot. This was to supply the torch flames for the gun fuses. I blew the charcoal to a ruddy glow, the chain shot was placed in the fire and the ladles stood by the pot. We were going into action, real action and a real challenge, not against a clumsy scow of a ship but a beauty like ourselves. She was flaunting the royal colors from the mainmast. We were dancing the American flag from our mainstaff.

What an unbelievable situation! A little American schooner from Perth Amboy, Woodbridge, and *Blazing Star* up against an American-built British schooner manned perhaps by people we might even know. What would be the outcome of this terrifying day?

Fear now returned to me and my teeth began to chatter. I couldn't prevent the beads of cold sweat from standing out on my forehead. As the moments fled by, my thoughts were of my mother — her kindness, her constant sacrifices for me, her desire for me some day to be a physician. She had written me recently that when the war was terminated,

---

*By the time of the War of 1812 these were called boarding axes. The handles were longer and the axes were used to chop rigging.

there would be a medical course given over at the little college in New Brunswick. How convenient that would be! It was all the more reason why I must survive. Fear left me now as the action closed. Anger returned. How could our neighbors do such a thing as this? Perhaps they would strike their colors without a fight. Perhaps they too were seized by fear, knowing full well our reputation. But we had no such good luck, for they were still coming on. We were heading right into each other. Our captain wasn't swerving his course the least bit. We would most certainly crash.

As we approached, I heard the captain of the other ship say, "This is your last chance to surrender, Hunter." I knew this disrespect would rile our captain. I turned and looked at him. He was furious. The vessels on his temples and forehead stood out and pulsated like angry writhing serpents. He nodded his head. Mr. Cook was in the foretop rigging and I realized I had been tardy on my job. I scampered up to the maintop. The captain nodded his head again and our two guns over the bow blasted out with hot-shot, striking the *Mistress* through her fore and mainsail. In an instant, they were on fire.

She quickly altered course to her starboard, either to avoid a collision, or to give us a broadside. With her six guns on a side, it was important that we not present our side or stern. We swerved quickly and our bow followed toward her stern. We reloaded and both guns spoke again over the bow. This time our shot was a little high and passed over her deck. Her three guns in the stern port now belched fire and it seemed eternity before they hit us on the larboard bow and I heard wood splinter. I stood as motionless as stone and just as cold. We swerved to our starboard to bring our larboard guns into range of her stern ports. Both our side carronades belched hot-shot directly into her stern windows. Part of her counter was carried away and immediately was on fire. She was constructed light all right, at least in the counter. There was a hurrah from our deck and a scamper from theirs. By two shots we had put her stern guns out of action. The stern shots from her first fire had hit our bow on an angle and bounced away, only splintering some planking. Meanwhile, their burning sails set off some powder and this added to the confusion. I looked at Mr. Cook. He pointed and called his shot. His aim was deadly. He picked the first man away from the gun on her larboard side. I took careful aim at a man who was about to light a torch from the pot. There was a terrific explosion from the pan and the barrel of my musket. I must have overloaded her for the shot knocked him down. He grabbed his side and reeled on the deck. The men were now afraid to go to their guns; they began to scamper into the rigging to escape or shoot at us as we reloaded the bow guns. They were evidently attempting to pick our men from the guns. As the first fellow ascended the maintop, there was another explosion from Mr. Cook's rifle; the fellow toppled over the railing and fell to the deck. I turned away. The other men quickly descended from the rigging or slid down lines, losing their guns overboard as they came down. They were running around aimlessly. The captain was urging them at pistol point to return to their guns. His men finally returned and reloaded. We passed on under her stern. She was on fire astern and the last of her sails were smoldering. Part of the crew was trying to put out the fire, and as far as maneuvering was concerned, she was helpless. Her rudder was carried away and we could see the buckets going overboard for water. It was most important to get the men at the guns and we were getting them. We knew their six starboard guns were loaded. If we could only pick the men away from these guns, we could prevent their fire. Only a torch bearer needed to strike the fuses, but they stood midships over the pot with the torches in their hands, paralyzed with fear and afraid to move. We sailed on under her counter and up on the starboard side. As we did, their four men ran forward and hit the fuses. We stood breathless, waiting for the momentary crash. It came and it was terrible!

It carried away our larboard and fife rails and down came the mainsail, crashing on the deck near where two of our men lay quietly. The captain jumped down from the poop deck, grabbed a torch, ran to our two guns and fired. He then hit the trough on the fire rail. Many of their men fell to the deck. This encouraged our men to return to the other gun and they fired, too. The result was breathtaking. It unseated two guns on the deck of the *King's Mistress.* Our guns killed five or six men. As they lay bleeding on the deck, the bloody pools grew larger and darker. The men were still.

I was so excited, I only stared. I didn't know what to do next. I looked forward and there stood Mr. Cook, who waved his hand coolly and pointed down to their captain. At that moment, their captain spotted ours. He leaned down on one knee, leveled his pistol over his arm and fired. The ball knocked off our captain's cockade, but Mr. Cook returned the fire so quickly, it seemed that the two went off almost together. Their captain sprawled out on the deck.

"For God's sake, strike the colors!" cried their men.

I looked down on our deck, but I couldn't see who the wounded men were. Most of our men on the deck were bleeding, but they were fighting on and fighting furiously. Mr. Irons, a big man, picked up a keg of powder and heaved it across onto their quarter deck. It landed right in the fire pot and the men scattered like so many rats. There resulted a terrible explosion, and she was now really on fire.

"Strike the colors!" cried the men. "We give up!"

She was so on fire that we couldn't stay by her side. The danger of a terrific explosion was momentary. In our injured condition, we drifted and half sailed away from her. We called to their men to have courage and jump, that we would pick them up, to lower their gig and get their captain in. But there was no use. Their captain was gone. We weren't pulling away from her fast enough, and with our shortened sail, we'd never make it. The fire was now

*135*

enveloping her entire stern. As it surged about the captain, we again saw that there was no sign of life, or motion. We called to the men as they were getting into the gig. There seemed to be about eight survivors.

"Where is your powder located?"

"Forward." Thank God, I thought.

"Pull for your life. Pull away as fast as you can. What about your wounded?" our men called.

"We are the wounded. The others are dead," they shouted back.

When we had drawn about an eighth of a mile away and felt that we were at a safe distance, we stood to. She was now in a mass of flames, which were travelling up her rigging. As the lines were consumed, the spars and topsails fell in flames, but the British flag was still flying. From the direction of the wind, we could still feel the heat. We lay to, allowing the men in the gig to overtake us, and we took them aboard. They leaned against the rail or sat down, heads in hands.

Some looked back and watched her burn. They were very still. There were a lot of privateers coming out of the inlet now, sailing directly toward us. I thought as I stood there, it might have been us.

Yes, it might have been us—except that from the first time we put into Little Egg Harbor until the present moment, we had trained, drilled, practiced. We had tried to think of all possible situations, how conditions might change, and what our reaction might be to any and all conditions. The captain had handpicked this crew and we had all cast our lot together as friends. Except in the heat of battle when the captain and the mates were in complete control, we all had the opportunity to express our opinions.

I was a little ashamed of myself, for I reflected that on a number of occasions I was actually standing on the far side of the mast watching the engagement. I believe, more than once, the captain, even in the heat of battle, was coolly calling up to me to pick this fellow or that fellow away from a gun. As I stood there reminiscing, there was a violent convulsive puff, followed by an earsplitting bang! The *Mistress* broke apart and slipped beneath the waves. She did not go down gloriously with her colors flying; the fiery mainmast was blown out of the hole and, as it arched across the sky with the colors upside down, it fell to the side and dipped its colors into the sea.

The men looked for a long while in the direction of the debris. What a fine ship she had been! The little fleet of privateers was now close by. Many men were in the rigging and, as they sailed up, they fired pistols and muskets and dipped their colors in our honor. In the excitement, more than one man fell overboard. And the little ships had to lay to and pick them up.

This was another failure for Sir Henry Clinton. All he could do now was storm and threaten, and increase the bounty on our little ship.

We had nothing to do with our prisoners of war; they were worse than Britishers in our minds. They were Americans, neighbors, who had turned against us and, as I later learned, two members of that crew who died that day were actually related to Rahway, Perth Amboy and Woodbridge men. One of those lost was the brother of one of our crew. The captain of the *King's Mistress* had been one Solomon Handy, and the correct name of the schooner was the *Dolly Hammill.*

It seems that there had been a personal feud between our good captain and theirs, for our captain had married the girl whom this other captain had courted. The feud had continued throughout the years. And when Clinton was desirous of obtaining a ship to take the *Blazing Star,* Handy had volunteered his services and supervised the construction. Their big mistake was that in order to sail as fast as we and carry such heavier armament, it was necessary to construct her lighter.

We proceeded, at the head of a parade, on back toward Little Egg. We weren't very happy now. All of the vigor, all of the hurrahs and jollification was aboard the other privateers. We were all guilty of having killed our fellow countrymen. We turned our attention to our wounded and one of them turned out to be Ed Hance. The captain examined him on the way in, having stopped the blood at the time of injury during the battle and probably saving his life. He had been wounded through the bowel. He lived, but throughout his lifetime he had an unpleasant opening on his side. The other man, Howard Hulse, had suffered a terrible concussion. Most of the other men had had splinters, cuts or fire burns.

The small number of people who now lived in the town of Little Egg assembled on the dock. I thought how wonderful it would have been if the destruction of the *Dolly Hammill* had occurred when Little Egg was at its heyday. What a reception we would have received. As it was, we tied up at the dock and took our prisoners ashore. They were promptly clapped into the town jail. Then we went directly back to our ship and began repairs. Except for the carrying away of the rail, the bow planking, and the destruction of a part of the fife rail, our damage wasn't too bad. Some of our sails were so damaged that they could not be repaired. But by and large, we were very fortunate, both our ship and our men. Mr. Springer and Mr. Purchase soon had the repairs well underway.

Many of the lesser wounds of our men were caused by splinters. We all agreed that Mr. Irons' act of throwing the keg of powder into the pot on the other ship had started her sure destruction, or led to the confusion which aided in her final destruction. The praises went round and round—the sight of the smiling Mr. Cook standing on the foretop, picking the men away from the guns with cold calculation, the sight of Mr. Pearsall standing alongside the captain, rapidly loading and firing a musket, the figure of the captain, who seemed to be everywhere. All recalled how he had dashed down the steps from the poop deck, grabbed up the pine knot and set off the two guns and the fire rail. His timely act had stimulated the men to return to the other gun and set it off. We all suddenly recalled that

Richard, and the men serving the beautiful brass stern gun, had no opportunity to use it, for we had never turned our counter toward this vessel.

It turned out that the reason our other guns were so well serviced (the starboard and larboard guns, which were turned from side to side and fired in pairs with chain shot and hot shot, together with the bow guns and swivel) was because the poop deck crew had come up and worked on the main deck. No one could remember who was responsible for turning us to our larboard after sailing under her stern. It was at that time we received the real damage from her broadside.

We all agreed that there was no individual glory. It turned out that Mr. Sykes, who always said he couldn't hit the broadside of a barn, had rarely fired his pistol, but when he did, he said he at least added to the confusion. Mr. Springer, who encouraged the men to stay at their guns, had helped make their firing a success. Mr. Purchase kept down the fire and, during the heat of the battle, made repairs to the lines and hawsers, and kept the deck clear. John Hunter and Howard Toms, who did most of the sailing during the battle, along with Louis Springer and Mr. Purchase, came in for special notice on their expert handling of the ship. At one moment these men were handling the ship and bringing her into line, and the next moment they were either firing muskets and pistols, or helping to service the guns. The captain expressed the opinion that as long as he lived, he would never expect to see a crew of sixteen men handle a ship so well, so skillfully and with so much battle wisdom.

Our adversary had been a schooner of 85 feet with a crew of 30 men. It was both sad and deplorable that out of this number only six men survived. The colors should have been struck earlier.

There is no doubt that Ed Cook saved our captain's life by shooting their captain when he had. He most certainly would have shot Captain Hunter had he been given another opportunity. Our captain was unmindful of the danger. No one recalled that during the battle he wasted any time cocking or firing a pistol, but the firing he did do contributed mightily to the final result. A carronade is deadly at short range!

Townspeople constantly came aboard—captains, mates, sailors, slaves, women and men, boys and girls of the town. They looked over every square inch of our ship and many of the girls were going below. They were paying particular attention to the men with the boundup wounds. Although I wasn't personally interested in any of the girls in the town, I almost wished that I had at least been hit by a flying splinter and could have had a wound bound up, too.

Mr. Cooke came along about this time and, with a twinkle and a smile, said, "Son, come down below and I'll pour ketchup all over you and bandage you up. Then the girls will pay attention to you."

I smiled, then laughed, and went about my work. But I mused that perhaps the people were wondering what I was doing during the battle. I made up my mind, that with the next fight I would distinguish myself in an outstanding manner. I was disturbed by one thing, that our captain, having been so successful in this last enterprise, might take on even greater ships to conquer. However, this time this thought did not cause any fear. I liken it to the fox hunt and the chase. If you have never jumped, you are seized with fear before the first, but after that they can't come fast enough. The thrill of sailing over a fence at great speed on a fine, young horse without change of pace is something you must experience to understand. And so, having gone through this battle, I was itching for the excitement of another engagement. The smell of powder, burning tar and pitch, the maneuvering into position, then the crashing of the guns, the cursing of the men, the cries of the wounded, the exhortations of the officers, the skillful handling of hot-shot by means of an iron ladle, seeing the men mowed down by the fire rail, the loading and firing of chain shot, watching it spin and tumble through the air, cutting down men and rigging, and then to see your adversary strike his colors; these are all vivid in my mind as though it were yesterday. I suppose it is the simple, basic, inevitable urge, from the earliest twilight of time—kill or be killed! Destroy or be destroyed!

# 14

*The summer of 1778* was one which I shall long remember. First there was the defeat of the *Dolly Hammill*. Second was the sudden evacuation of Philadelphia by Clinton due to the pressure by Washington and his generals. Then there was my approaching marriage in September. There was no way I could return to the Eastern Shore of Maryland and marry the girl I loved. So it was decided that she would come up to New Jersey and stay first with her relatives near Hopewell, and then come on and stay with my mother in Amboy, where we would be married in the little church on the hill.* The fourth thing which I shall long remember was the sudden disastrous depreciation of our currency, due in large part to the circulation (originally by Dunmoore in Virginia and by Clinton in New York) of counterfeit American paper money in enormous amounts.

    Clinton's retreat across New Jersey and his disaster at Monmouth Courthouse caused him to retreat to Sandy Hook Island, and from there he was taken off by Admiral Howe to New York. This clearly indicated how strongly Amboy and the towns along the sound were being controlled by New Jersey militiamen and Captain Edgar's Light Horse.

---

*St. Peter's Episcopal.

Our good captain was discussing the possibility of sailing directly back to Perth Amboy so that all of us could see our loved ones at home, have a much needed rest, and help get in the harvest. And so we began to make plans.

In the meanwhile, an ever increasing business was developing at Tuckerton. The bay and harbor were again filled with the masts of privateers and prizes. So as one looked across the harbor, it appeared very much like a new forest had grown up almost overnight. Prosperity was here and many new houses were going up. There was a brisk business in the sale of captured commodities and Tuckerton had become a thriving community rather than a village. The shift was from Little Egg and Chestnut Neck. A constant train of wagons passed back and forth across the marsh road, bringing in goods and taking out others purchased at the prize court auction. The prize court had been accepting paper money for these purchases. The first part of August, couriers brought word that the British were circulating counterfeit paper money throughout the colonies. When the prize courts sent the money on to Robert Morris, he found it was counterfeit.*

Early in the year, George III had been advised by Lord Amherst to withdraw all the British troops from Philadelphia and, in the event of an alliance between France and America, to evacuate New York and Rhode Island. But the depreciation of our currency, and the consequent poverty of our people without a government, revived the British hopes. On the other hand, the peace commissioners believed that if Clinton would give up Philadelphia, the colonies might return to English rule.

The United States closed the campaign of 1778 before autumn for want of money. Paper bills issued by Congress on the pledge of faith of each separate state supported the war during this period. Their depreciation was hastened by the repeated disasters which had befallen the American armies. Their value was further impaired by the guile of

---

*The money was largely made at the Rivington Press in New York Town.

British ministers, under whose authority Lord Dunmoore introduced into circulation in Virginia and other states over one million dollars in bills counterfeited in England.

In October, 1776, Congress, which did not possess power to levy taxes and had no power on which credit could be founded, opened loan offices in several of the states and authorized a lottery. In December it issued five million dollars more in continental bills. In January of 1777, when they had sunk to one-half of their pretended value, it denounced every person who would not receive them at par as a public enemy, liable to forfeit anything he offered for sale. It requested the state legislatures to declare the continental paper money a lawful tender. This Massachusetts had enacted a month before, and the example was followed throughout the other states.

The loan offices exchanged United States paper money at par for certificates of debt bearing six percent interest. On the hint from Arthur Lee, Congress resolved to pay this interest by drawing on its commissioners in Paris for coin. The bills were of a very long date and, before they became due, one dollar in coin was worth six in paper. I heard our men say they were glad they owned farms.

In the middle of November, 1776, Massachusetts, which had grown opulent before the war by tolerating no currency but hard money, proposed a convention of committees from several of the New England states to consider all questions relating to public credit. Connecticut feared the proposal would give umbrage to Congress. Upon this, a convention of the New England states was called by Rhode Island under the name of a Council of War and met on Christmas Day at Providence. They regulated prices, proposed taxation and loans, and recommended that the states should issue no more paper "unless in extreme cases." Congress liked their doings so much that on January of 1777, it advised similar conventions of the middle and three most southern states.

Congress was striving for its monopoly of paper money and asked the states to call in their bills and issue no more.

*144*

All the measures hitherto suggested had failed and Massachusetts once more took the lead. On her invitation, the four New England states and New York met near the end of July at Springfield on the Connecticut River. With one voice they found the root of all financial difficulties in the use of irredeemable paper and on this remedy they proposed to "sink" all bills of the states and to provide alike for their local expenses and those of the war by quarter-yearly taxes. The developments of the colonial institutions were promoted by showing how readily the people, the delegates from a group of states, could act together for the purposes of reform. But prices continued to rise and bills to go down. The anxious deliberations of the committee of Congress during more than two months at Yorktown, with the report of the Springfield convention before them, produced only a recommendation, adopted on the 22nd of November, 1777, that the several states should become creditors of the United States by raising for the Continental Congress treasury five million dollars in four quarterly installments. The first payment was to be made on the coming New Year's Day and the whole to bear six percent interest until the final adjustment of the accounts after the confederation had been ratified. I was fearful that my father would lose everything for which he had worked.

In May of 1778, the Congress wrote to the American people "the reason that your money hath depreciated is because no taxes have been imposed to carry on the war," but still it did not venture to ask the states to grant the power to levy taxes. Our commissioners in France and Spain were living on shadowy hopes of foreign loans, while the individuals throughout the thirteen states were waxing rich by buying and selling real estate, commodities, and livestock in return for hard money. Thus, having fought hard to capture, bring in prizes and auction them, we found about the first of August, 1778, that we were turning over only worthless paper money to our Congress.

The rich were getting richer and the poor were becoming poorer. The rich were acquiring that which is always valuable — land, homes, furniture, stock, plate, and other commodities of real value. The poor had a trunkful of paper for their tears, sweat and toil.

The British were now secure in New York, their armies having been successful in the South. In each instance they were living off the land. We noticed a definite drop of smuggled trading by Loyalists, refugees, and by ghost traders up and down the coast. The prizes were dropping off. The captains of the various privateers were gathering and discussing the next move. On the fifteenth of August, we sailed out of the inlet for home!

We followed the coastline closely until we passed Barnegat, but after that we turned sharply out to sea, for there were no more suitable inlets to dash into until Spermacetti, just this side of the Hook, and under the shadow of the Highlands of the Naversink (Navesink).

If we met a formidable enemy, it was either a question of running to sea or running back to Barnegat or Little Egg. We regulated our sailing time so that we would approach Spermacetti just before dark. And so, on the seventeenth of August, 1778, just at dusk, we sighted the great light on Sandy Hook Island. We sailed directly in toward the landfall until we saw the breakers, and then we sailed south along the breakers until we could see the breakers cease and the free running water through the inlet of Spermacetti. Entering the inlet and following it closely under the Highlands of the Naversink and on up Raritan Bay, we threw down the anchor off the old inn (Port Monmouth). The gig lowered, and the captain and six men went ashore, all heavily armed. We all stood along the rail, all of us armed. Richard looked like a pirate. His great bronze chest and muscles stood out above his ragged, knee-length breeches, but he wore his tricone like a general. In half an hour the captain returned and gave us all the news; all the harbors and the way home on this side of Staten Island were safe from large ships, except for an occasional British shallop or sloop from New York sailing around Staten Island investigating or spying. Our whale boats generally took care of them.

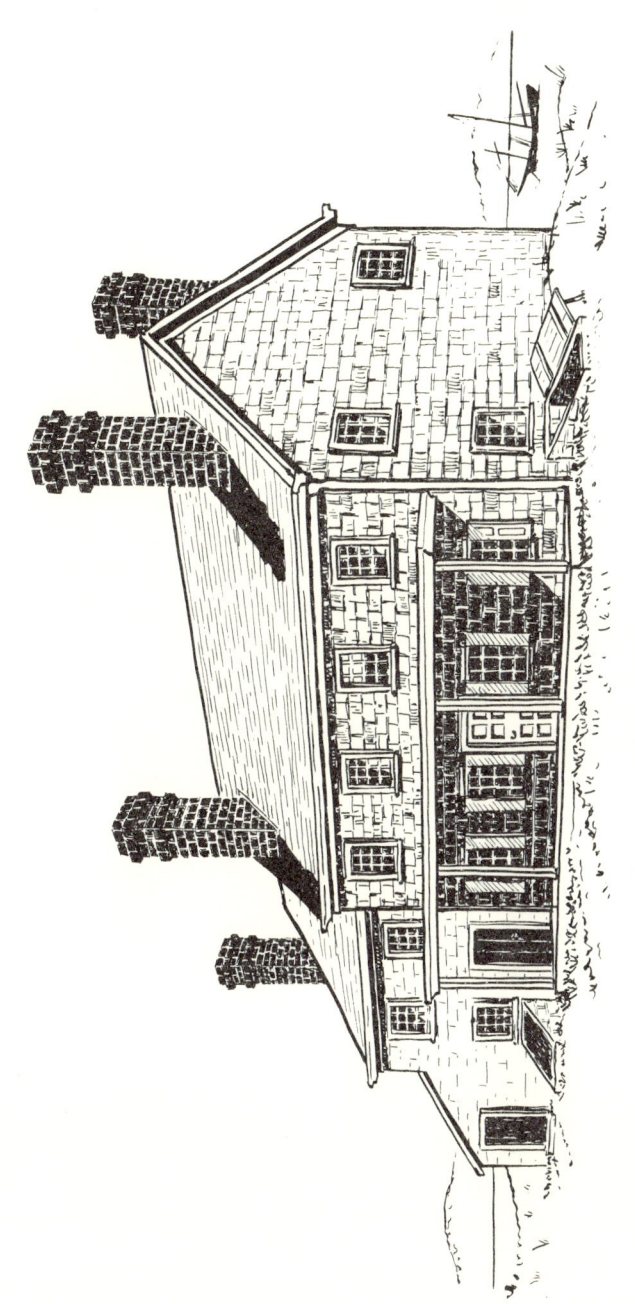

*The Old Inn, still an inn*

It wasn't safe, however, to lie here overnight. The captain pointed out the night lights of the Jersey, lying behind the tip of Sandy Hook. We hoisted anchor and, in the darkness, sailed on up the bay. Just before daybreak, we lay off the little creek separating Perth Amboy from Woodbridge and the hamlet of Blazing Star. It didn't seem possible, but we were now within a mile of home. In the early morning haze and semidarkness, we shortened sail to jib and mainsail and sailed up the creek. We tied up to the dock, at the back of the farm. I didn't even ask permission. I just jumped over the side and fled like a deer up the road toward home.

No one could see our schooner now, with the high marsh banks and the twisting creek, the tall marsh grass and overhanging branches of the trees. With the white sails removed, I don't think anyone could ever find it. The farm was surrounded on the one side by marshes and the other by deep forests. Furthermore, all the people in the immediate locality were either friends or relatives.

I fled on. A whale oil lamp was burning in my house. I later learned that my mother had a premonition that we were coming home, and on that very day had left a light burning. I grabbed the great door knob, but the door was locked. Not waiting to strike the knocker, I dashed around to the back, but it too was locked. I knocked softly and one of the slaves let me in.

In a moment I was in my mother's arms. Although she was a very stoic woman, she wept freely now and so did I. In a few moments there was a knock on the front door and, as it opened, my father appeared in the doorway. The embracing continued. I now made a tour of the house; it was just as I had left it only it seemed more beautiful than ever. Every piece of furniture, every drape, every candlestick, every pressed or sandwich glass lamp, every rug and carpet was in its place. I remembered them exactly as I had pictured them night after night as I lay in my bunk. I rubbed my hands over the wainscoting, the chairs, and the tables. In a very short while we were sitting down to breakfast and the discussion was all about my coming marriage.

Three years before, I had gone away a boy, and now I was a man. My father was discussing how we would divide the farm, but I would have no part of that. We would all live together on the same great farm. Perhaps I would follow the sea, at least coastwise, after this terrible conflict was over. My mother said I would study medicine. Then I wondered if it would ever be over. But my father assured me it was very close to being over, for after the disaster at Monmouth, the British peace commissioners were meeting regularly in Philadelphia. The government of New York was holding out for independence, supported by New England and New Jersey, and they were receiving more support daily. France was trying to influence us to return to the Crown. Spain was fearful of our nation becoming independent lest the same thing happen in her own country and this, too, was worrying France. Catherine of Russia said, "No telling where these crazy ideas of the rights of man, the common man, the loss of respect for nobility, might end."

Reports had come out that the three commissioners representing England were favorable to the colonies, and had already sent reports back to George III that we could not be conquered. They recommended that England should take any method, even appeasement, to draw us back to the Crown; and that if the Crown missed this opportunity for reconciliation, there would be no reconciliation ever.

I went to bed thinking of my dear Helen so far away. I was proud of my home, our farm, my people and their accomplishments. The people of New Jersey did not live on as grand a scale as the people in Maryland, but our living was comparable to the best in this locality. I wished the marriage ceremony was over, sure I could never stand up to it. My knees would buckle and I would probably collapse as I stood in the chancel of the church, waiting for my dear one to come up the aisle. Then my thoughts returned to her beauty and how she stood in the doorway of the store that memorable first morning.

The days went by rapidly. There was scarcely enough time left before the wedding for me to do the daily farm work. The farm was in fine shape. The additional slaves which had descended upon us, as their Tory, Loyalist or refugee masters fled, were making us very prosperous. There were enough men to work in the sawmill and the cabinet shop, where we had always turned out some of the finest furniture in this section. We had enough men to repair and paint the buildings, to care for the farm and the stock. We were preparing to drive a large flock of sheep, cattle, and hogs by wagon, to General Washington, who was in winter quarters at Middlebrook.

I was so busy all day and so tired at night that I hardly had little opportunity to think. One Monday I woke with a start and realized that this was the day, September 1, 1778 – my wedding day.

There is no use trying to remember what took place on that day. I do remember I was placed in the chancel and I remember how beautiful my loved one looked. I remember the smile on Mr. Fitzgerald's face as he escorted his daughter up the aisle. Her mother and father had come up from Maryland the day before and were staying at our home. I remember vaguely the reception at home. I remember how the families tried to chase us off to bed and finally, when they did not succeed and we sat talking, looking at old books, albums, the family Bible, and making entries in it, in despair they gave up and went off to bed themselves. Sometime later, about midnight, we retired.

It seemed the most natural thing to be together. In the morning we arose early, had an early breakfast, and took our walk down to the good ship. Mr. Pearsall had no immediate family, so he elected to stay on *Blazing Star*. He seemed very happy there. Although on many occasions we invited him to stay at the farm, he graciously refused and it was clear that he preferred to stay aboard the trim little vessel.

Mr. Hance went home for about two weeks, as did Mr. Irons and Mr. Orange. In fact, all three went down to Barnegat together and came back together. Then they too remained aboard ship. They offered to help with the crops, but they remarked with a laugh that they probably wouldn't know hay from weeds. And it was better for them to be guarding the ship anyway. Mr. Cook helped tremendously about the farm, however, and I remember Mr. Pearsall came up and took care of the chickens occasionally, when some of the farm help were away; he loved chicken, both alive and in the pot.

On Sundays, Helen and I went to church and on Saturdays, we went to town. During the week I worked hard on the farm, in the cabinet shop and in the sawmill. My father was a stickler for never allowing anything to run down. He had a hawk's eye for anything in disrepair.

The month of September passed rapidly and the month of October just as quickly. Our slaves were not allowed to go down through the woods to our ship. We were afraid they might talk in town, so this area was completely taboo. We told them of ghouls, goblins, and demons living in the marshes and the wood and an old haunted cemetery. None of them ever went near the ship.

On several occasions, my dear one and I walked through the woods and along the banks of the creek to ascertain if our little vessel could be seen from any direction, for the leaves were dropping now, but never were we able to see her, not even with a glass. This was the most perfect act of deception I had ever seen. In fact, the vessel was so cleverly hidden that before we set sail, it was necessary to cut away many branches which had grown out, even after our arrival home in August.

It was a beautiful long fall and I never saw the farm more beautiful nor in finer shape. When we went down to our little vessel, we found that the men aboard had put her in fine shape. Meanwhile we were all busy collecting shot, powder, fuses, charcoal and provisions. The women had been busy making and repairing sails, making good warm winter clothing and uniforms. The men who lived aboard the ship made quite a thing of coming up to the house and being fitted for their uniforms. Though they joked about it, they were very proud.

As the fall went on, many of us went hunting and brought in much game — quail, pheasant, wild turkey, deer, ducks and geese, and an abundance of rabbits. They were put down in the ice house. With the wood supply more than adequate at the kitchen door, and the farm fields prepared for spring, the winter grain sown in, the barns filled almost to bulging, the stock in fine shape, with all the comforts of the family provided, and the promised livestock sent to General George Washington, our captain was becoming restless to leave. My dear Helen and I made a trip behind a fast high-stepping gelding to Cranesford to see if Mr. Sykes was ready, to Rahway to see if the Springers were ready, and Woodbridge to notify Mr. Thoms.

On the first day of November I was sent around the circuit again to determine whether the men would be ready by the fifth. I returned and told the captain that the men would be coming down before that time.

After the usual fond embraces, all the men assembled on the fourth of November and we rode off up the Perth Amboy-Woodbridge Road, which was in the opposite direction to our ship. We entered our woods from the far side on the Woodbridge line, came on down through the old woods road and went aboard.

I recall that I had promised that I would follow the sea with the captain after the war was over, but now that I was leaving my dear Helen, I was sure that I would not do that at all after the war was over. We cut away the branches, told the driver of the wagon that he could have the day off and go on to Rahway if he wished, but not to return before nightfall to the farm, for we wanted the black help and slaves to believe that the ship was a great distance away.

There was a heavy, low hanging fog that cool November morning and so we felt our way down the creek and into the sound. By dead reckoning we reached Raritan Bay. The fog was lifting slightly and we could see the heights of Perth Amboy. The wind was not increasing, so we knew the fog would hold for a while longer. We clapped on all the sails. The tide was running out, so it was in our favor. We continued down the bay. The wind now increased and the fog rapidly dissipated. By the time we arrived at the inn (at Port Monmouth), the fog had entirely lifted. This inn was kept by an old friend of Captain Hunter, an old waterfront fellow by the name of Bradford Johnson, a loyal patriot from a good Monmouth family. The day was brisk and cold, and the wind was strong. As we shortened sail and prepared to drop anchor, Brad was out on the front lawn, beckoning to us in a most alarming manner. This time the captain took Mr. Cook, who had already lowered the gig, Mr. Pearsall, and myself ashore. As soon as we stepped onto the beach, Brad told us there was a British shallop, 35 or 40 feet long, cruising along under the Highlands of the Naversink, and coming ashore at times to get information. He said his men had shot two refugees and thrown them into the bay just the week before for supplying information to the British. This shallop had put ashore at the inn to get some grog and he had had an opportunity to inspect her. She had one swivel on the bow, a good size gun, probably a five-pounder, and about 16 well armed men for the crew. They seemed to be sailor-soldiers. We asked Bradford where he had seen them last. He believed they had laid near Spermacetti Cove the night before.

We walked into the inn and how lovely it was. The long fireplace contained two briskly burning stumps in which you could have stood a horse. It looked like the kind of inn that pirates might frequent. The building must have been 125 years old. The hand oiled and rubbed paneling of the taproom and the wainscoting about the wall added to its charm. The beautiful Dutch and English plates on the plate rail, and the silver, copper and pewter tankards on the rack behind the bar, and the wide board floors, grooved and hollowed, ridged and wavy from the years of tramping and dancing by men in sea boots, enhanced its beauty. We had an ale, thanked Brad, and departed, carrying ample ale back to the ship for our men. Then we weighed anchor and proceeded down the bay.

We could have gone straight out the inlet, but the bow watch spotted the British shallop lying by the water hole at Water Witch. The captain called to the men. "What shall we do with the shallop, men?"

"Take her," they cried in unison.

The decision was made. The shallop was getting up her sails now. Certainly she would not attempt to engage us. I had no desire to meet sixteen experienced sailors or soldiers of the British navy on the deck of our ship, but we were certain we could stand her off and at a distance we could thrash her. She was standing off the beach now, pointing directly toward us. She loaded her bow gun as a precaution, but when she was about a quarter of a mile away, we hoisted our flag. She went about quickly and fled toward the mouth of the Naversink. We clapped on everything in the way of sails in order to catch her before she made the turn under the Highlands of the Naversink, for there might be a fleet of them there.

We knew that we dare not pursue her up that shallow narrow body of water. The distance between us was closing very rapidly. We had the advantage of being further offshore and thus received a more favorable wind since the wind was from the west and cut off by the Highlands of the Naversink. I now realized that she had stood off that beach in order to get more wind, but she had not stood off far enough.

The captain ordered the two bow guns fired.* They were loaded and rammed home well. Pine knot torches were hurried from the pot and the fuses were stuck in the touch holes. There was a tremendous report (as the torches struck the fuses), echoing up and down beneath the Highlands. The water fowl flew off in screeching alarm. The shots were well placed and landed on either side of her. However, she continued onward. She was almost at the point where she could make her turn. There she would be safe. But here

---

*These guns were not directed forward but rather quarter forward.

she might lose the wind entirely, so the oars were going out. Yet we were flying on and closing the gap rapidly.

We now paralleled her. The starboard bow gun was swung around to aid the two side guns, the larboard gun having been brought to the side of the starboard. There were now three guns on the one side — the regular starboard gun, the larboard gun which had been brought over, and the bow gun which had been swung to the side.

We were abreast of her now. Her men were rowing furiously, and now turning toward the beach. Our men took careful aim, concentrating the three guns... and then they fired. I couldn't tell whether she was hit by one ball or two, but all activity on the shallop stopped at once. Presently we could see she was awash and the gunwhale was going under. The shallop would never make it to the beach and the clothing of the men was too heavy for them to swim ashore. We headed about and moved in toward them as rapidly as possible. At the same time we lowered the gig. Our ship was still moving faster than the men in our gig could row, so we did not cut it free. As we sailed up alongside of her, we realized we were too late. Only two men of the entire crew survived; some had been hit and some had drowned. The two were clinging to the wreckage and our men hauled them aboard. They were both Irishmen. Eddie Cook asked them why they were fighting for the King of England and what they expected to get for it. Mr. Pearsall remarked, "Some day you'll be fighting for your own independence."

We asked them if there were any other British ships in the locality, and they replied, "Only the *Jersey*," pointing in her direction. Through their glasses, the crew on the *Jersey* must have seen what had happened. But there was nothing they could do about it, even if she had a full crew, for she was as clumsy as a Dutch shoe.

We went about quickly and headed on out through Spermacetti Inlet, on down the coast for Little Egg. We wanted to give the two Irishmen the run of the ship, but they were surly and sullen. They called us a dirty, stinking bunch of Protestant Reformers. We laughed because they were worse off than we were. They were fighting for Protestant Reformers. We clapped them into irons and spiked them in the hold.

The weather was still fair, the wind strong and out of the west. We sailed along on the quarter, only a short distance beyond the breakers, for from Sandy Hook to Barnegat there are no shoals close to shore, but at Barnegat even a shoal draft boat must stand off at least two miles.

By sailing close to the shore, we had the advantage of the wind without the sloppy chop of the sea. By nightfall we were passing beyond Barnegat. We could have sailed in the inlet at Barnegat and proceeded down the bay, but the bay below the inlet is so twisting, winding and shallow at points that no one but a fool would venture there after dark, for to go aground would invite an attack by Barnegat Pirates or Pine Robbers. So we continued down outside now about four miles at sea. The wind slackened off at sunset. It would come up again after sunset, we hoped, in the same direction. We didn't mind that it had slackened off because we did not wish to reach Little Egg before daylight.

During the early evening, the wind increased slightly coming out of the northwest, and at daybreak we stood into the inlet at Little Egg. We were back among friends. It seemed like our second home. We dropped anchor, sent the two manacled Irishmen ashore, took in the sails and went down to supper. While we sat at the table eating, we discussed customs, superstitions and traditions.

But soon it was getting late and the men were tired. We had had a hard day. So one by one we filed off to bed.

My thoughts naturally led back to my home, to my dear wife, and the joyful thought which she had very modestly told me, as we parted, that we were going to have a baby. I hoped that it would be a boy, but it did not matter much. I lay there in my bunk, thinking how happy I was and wondering what they were doing at home, and how happy my dear one seemed to be. She was so far away from her old home on the Manokin River, but she seemed very happy. I was too tired to write tonight, but I would write tomorrow. And so I fell asleep.

In the morning, the captains came aboard. They told us that the Barnegat Pirates were up to their old tricks. During the change of seasons, from summer to fall, with the increase in the violence of the winds, storms and fogs, they had, in their well known way, caused several wrecks on the beach. The militia had come over in an attempt to capture them, but without much success. Something would have to be done.

The most notorious of these Barnegat Pirate wrecks occurred on the fifteenth of December, 1778. They had wrecked the brig *Perseverance* bound from Havre to New York with Captain Snow, ten passengers and a crew of seven men. This occurred below Barnegat Light and I quote the exact description from the newspaper published at Parkerstown on Friday, the day before she was "cast away":

"A ship from New York was spoken, which deceived them by stating they were east of Sandy Hook. It was with great gratification that the passengers received this joyous news and, elated with the hope of soon resting on terra firma, gave themselves up to hilarity and merriment while the captain, under the same impulse, spread all sail to a heavy northeaster with the high expectations of a safe arrival on the morrow (at New York). Delusive hope — tomorrow too many were destined never to see. Thus she continued on her course until three o'clock Saturday morning when the mate who was watching on deck was heard to give the dreadful cry ... 'Breakers ahead!' The brig, by the instant efforts of her steersmen, obeyed her helm, but as she came around to head off shore, her stern striking bottom knocked off her false keel, deadened her headway and she backed on the beach, stern foremost. In less than fifteen minutes the sea made a clear breech over her. ... Passengers rushed out of the cabin, some of them in their night clothes; six of them and two of the crew got in the long boat. One of these was a French lady of great beauty. The remainder of the crew succeeded in reaching the roundtop, excepting a Mr. Cologne, whose great weight and corpulence of person compelled him to remain in the shrouds. Soon the sea carried the long boat and its passengers clear of the wreck. When it was too late, it was discovered she was firmly attached to it by a hawser which it was impossible to separate. Had it not been for this unfortunate circumstance, they might have possibly reached the shore. Their cries were heart-rending, but were soon silenced in the sleep of death. The boat swamped and they were all consigned to one common grave. The body of the lady floated on shore. The sea ran so high that it wet those on the roundtop, and although many efforts were made on Saturday, it was found impossible, as the boats would upset by turning head over stern, subjecting those in them to great danger. Captain Snow lost his life in attempting to swim to shore. On Sunday the sea fell a little, and those on the wreck were made to understand they would have to build a raft of the spars and get on it, or they could not be saved. The mate had fortunately secured a hatchet, with which one was constructed, by which the survivors ... reached the shore in safety. There were but four saved out of the seventeen souls on board, that is, one passenger that was badly frozen, the mate and two of the crew ... three perished on the round-top or were thrown over. Mr. Cologne, who was in the rigging and unable to descend from the shrouds, let go and fell into the water, and was caught as he came up by his hair and thus towed ashore. He lived only three days after, although every possible attention was paid him. He and his niece, the young French lady, were buried side by side in the Golden Burying Grounds at our point."

An investigation of the facts, as our good captain and the other privateer captains in the harbor conducted at the Customs House, indicated some high smelling skunkery. In the first place, who was and why did this ship at sea deliberately give these people false directions? If this was a legitimate wreck, why wasn't the town of Parkerstown so notified? There was more than one little ship in this harbor which would have sailed out and aided this particular ship, regardless of the fact that its cargo was going to Clinton in New York.

The most shocking thing of all is the fact that in the editorial of our local paper, the editor attempted to defend the people who did the pirating. There is no telling how extensive, how widespread, and how devious were the ramifications of the people involved as Barnegat Pirates, Pine Robbers, and Pine Barons, and their relationship to the very neighbors in the town.

This spoiled for us what might have been a quiet but pleasant Christmas. This could have occurred to my dear one, had she and her family come up by boat. This could have happened to any of our friends and close relatives, for many of them traveled to the South and even hazarded an occasional trip northward to the New England colonies to visit their relatives. This is merely an example of what was going on throughout this entire period.

The depreciation of currency by counterfeiting, the profiteering by people who had hard money, the privateering by Loyalists against our privateers, the regiments and companies of refugees, made up of our own people fighting our own people, the maurading and killing by the Pine Barons, the theft of property and destruction of human life by the Barnegat Pirates, all were making our fight for freedom precarious, and Parkerstown was becoming rich.

# 15

*Our work was* now settling down to a humdrum routine. We were bringing in the prize ships, but then we weren't doing any more than the other privateers. What we couldn't bring in, we burned, after stripping them and taking what we could use. Occasionally we weakened. When we found a repentant captain who signed the book that he would not deal with the enemy and that he would return to his home port, we sometimes turned him loose. This depended upon his reputation before the war. But when we captured ships composed of refugees or questionable characters, when we suspected them of being Barnegat Pirates, or when they were distinctly British or favorable to the British, as the Quakers were apt to be, we took them in and frequently sold their ships. Then their ships sailed forth under our flag.

As the coastwise trade dwindled again, due to our increased activity, we would sail up the coast in small packs and completely destroy the fishing fleets out of New York, because they were supplying the British with food. We liked particularly to sail up the night before, or leave Little Egg the day before, sail throughout the night, arrive off New York in fog, and then in the early morning fog or as the fog lifted, seize these fishing boats and destroy them.

Frequently we would put their captains ashore in their whale boats; many of these men we knew.

The most important and joyful news that I received throughout the year came in by courier about the first of July. On the sixth of June, 1779, I became the father of a healthy, robust son. We had a fine party on shipboard and Ed Cook said he didn't think I had it in me!

Although our captain took only a very small part of the prize money for our working capital, we were becoming rich, and so it was decided that we would take an even smaller portion. Hessian deserters, British deserters, and Scotch deserters were buying land and settling all around Amboy, Woodbridge, Rahway, and Metuchen. A great deal of this land was still owned by our family. It seemed so incongruous that our men had suffered so in camp this past winter while we were so comfortable. We had everything we wished.

Regardless of how much we sent to our great general's army in the way of captured blankets, clothes, shoes, stockings, scarves, and so forth, the army was like a great sprawling baby, never satisfied and always calling for more. We knew there must be something wrong with the organization. We knew there must be pilfering and actual theft on a large scale. Everyone in the churches, in the schools, and aboard the ships was sending things to turn into money to buy food, obtain clothing, or to turn into what other little comforts the army required. We supplied them with choice liquor, beer, wine, and rum from the captured ships, but the baby still cried for more, and we bent our backs to provide more. To read the newspapers, the situation was very confusing. The army was still in need!

At this time we got some consolation from all the newspaper accounts. One thing was certain. The British were avoiding Amboy, Woodbridge, Rahway, Elizabethtown, New Brunswick, and Cranesford*, from which most of our crew came. Of course, except for the one excursion

---

*Cranford

into Little Egg they had never molested the county of Mr. Irons, Mr. Orange, Mr. Hance, and Mr. Purchase, Monmouth. But then their county was infected by something worse—the Refugees, Loyalists, Pine Barons, and Barnegat Pirates.

# 16

*The year 1779* dragged on with almost unbearable monotony. I longed for my wife and baby, my family and my home. I thought often of the farm, my town, my church, my old friends. I wondered where they might be. I felt certain that none of us could ever take up where we had left off; things had changed too much.

As the year drew to a close, the weather was becoming very violent, so we put into Little Egg, fearful that we might be excluded from any of the other inlets by the packing of ice.

Christmas was a dull one because our families dared not risk crossing the Pine Barrens. There was no danger to our loved ones at home, since the British avoided that area. But they dared not venture southward through the open country across the Pine Barrens to Little Egg. The Pine Barons, the Pine Robbers, the Barnegat Pirates, the Refugees, and the Loyalists were much more active than they had ever been. This was undoubtedly due to our bringing in so many prizes. So much material was going inland that the pickings now were very choice. Then, too, our armies were now so far flung. They were fighting for the colonies in the South, holding Clinton bottled up in New York, fighting on the broad frontiers of New England, Western New York, and

Pennsylvania. The fine work of General Sullivan and of Major Ayres,* protecting the frontiers, resulted in less available protection for the people in this section and along the eastern coastline of the state.

Thus we spent a dull Christmas at Little Egg. With the great growth of Parkerstown, the many evidences of wealth among the local people, the aloofness of these people, we now knew not which of them were our friends. We were not even certain how many friends we had on other ships. We were not certain how many of these captains were turning over the money, the goods, and the money returned from the sale of goods, to Robert Morris and the army. We could not be certain whether some of the privateers were not privateering for themselves.

---

*Charles William Gilman, M.D., of Woodbridge, N.J.

# 17

*We spent long* periods at sea and the monotony of the constant routine was beginning to get us all down. The year 1782 was drawing rapidly to a close. These last three years had been years of unbearable routine with the most intense homesickness. The war was becoming a stalemate. When we met great ships of the line, we fled; when we met lesser ones, we took them. The longing for home was noticeable in all our men. I believe our good captain made no attempt to go home for fear he would not go to sea again. As long as we stayed away, we could keep going, but if we returned home for even so short a visit as just a few days, we might not find ourselves able to continue in the same old humdrum manner, regardless of how much our country needed us.

To make matters worse, there had been constant meetings between the British commissioners and Congress relative to a peace. As early as 1779 it looked as though we might have peace, but then we couldn't agree on the fisheries and the boundaries. And so the war dragged on. Clinton was bottled up in New York by our great General Washington. The British fleet lay in the harbor, as much to evacuate the British suddenly as to guard against the French fleet entering the harbor. The French fleet was now at Newport.

The fighting had been going on furiously in the South with the victories in the beginning to the British, but as time went on, Cornwallis was gradually being pushed back into Virginia. The constant harassing of his rear guard and of his flanks by the young, vigorous, staunch patriots, Lafayette and Greene, not to forget Marion, Sumpter, and Shelby on the frontier, had finally caused Cornwallis to retreat down the peninsula in Virginia, down to Yorktown. Here he was rimmed on the north, west and south by the French and Continental armies. His fleet had failed him; Clinton never came to help.

What would they do now and where could they go? They had failed in New England. They had failed in the Middle states; they were failing in the South.

Intercepted communications over a long period of time, and reports from Franklin in Europe, told of the jealousy between Cornwallis and Clinton, and the dissatisfaction of both over a successful termination of this war. On one occasion Clinton wrote:

> "This army (American) is often defeated, only to go on and reorganize during the night and set up advantageous and harassing positions to our gallant army. They have led us up and down the length and breadth of this country, and when we feel we have defeated them, they pop up somewhere else, and harass another one of our garrisons."

On the twentieth of August, 1782, we were proceeding northward on the Atlantic Ocean, perhaps 50 miles at sea. The bow look-out, and Mr. Cook in the foretop, cried out almost at the same time that there was a vast fleet aproaching from the north. Our first inclination was to turn and fly, but then we realized that information concerning this fleet should be obtained and passed on to our general. In half an hour we could see that this was a veritable armada. In another half hour, to our great pleasure, by its royal ensign, we saw it was the fleet of De Grasse. Why had it left Newport? Where was it going? God grant that it wasn't going back to the West Indies to refit! We sailed toward it, slackened sail, and watched it go by.

It was led by small frigates, schooners, and gun boats, followed by great proud ships of the line, four deckers of 64 and 74 guns. It was at least an hour and a half in passing. We stood proudly by. This indeed was an opportunity of a lifetime. How many sailors would ever see such a magnificent armada passing in review? We were proud as we sailed back and forth, exalted to have such an ally. We were highly pleased that we were flying our little flag at the masthead, that beautiful American flag and I looked up at it many times. I have seen the colors of many nations in my lifetime, yet never any as beautiful as the colors of this, the American flag. It was not the copy or modification of any other nation. It was original, both in its idea and its design. Thirteen stars in a blue field signified a new constellation in the sky of nations.

The fleet passed onward and disappeared down beyond the horizon. We sailed on in the hope of capturing a suitable prize, but pickings were difficult now. The fishermen refused to come out of New York and work the banks, and the captains who had traded with the British had long since given up. The risk was too great and the losses too certain. We went on through October and into November; it was beginning to be very cold. The weather was nasty almost continuously. The sea was becoming more violent daily. The long ridges of water were taller and steeper and snow flurries had come early. On one occasion we were so close to New York that we were tempted to slip home. But we knew that at this time of year the risk was too great. With the leaves off the trees, our ship would most certainly be seen from Staten Island. And with the intense hatred of us, there would undoubtedly be a special expedition organized. They not only would destroy our little ship, but they would destroy our farms and perhaps our families. So we thought better of it, and sailed southward, farther and farther from home.

Having seen no ships, in need of provisions and fresh water, and because the weather was rapidly closing in and becoming very cold, on the first of December, the captain decided to head back to Little Egg. We had just gone about. Suddenly there was a cry from the man in the maintop calling out that a great merchant ship was on the horizon. Soon the cry was repeated that it was coming our way. Every man went to his station and we headed toward this great ship. Ordinarily we would have avoided such a ship, but the pickings had been bad for a long time. The wind was blowing from the northeast at about 25 miles an hour. There were many snow clouds collecting in the sky and the velocity of the wind was increasing. With it there was an occasional snow flurry. As the ship bore rapidly down toward us, we sailed toward her as cautiously as our first time out. Every man stood motionless at his station as we approached within spyglass distance. Suddenly the man on watch in the maintop cried out that they were uncovering many deck guns. The captain shouted, "Ready—about!" We spun on our keel, momentarily stopping the onrushing seas as we rolled. We clapped on everything from the sail locker, except the tablecloth. We must have looked like all sail and no boat.

The charts were called and our course plotted for Little Egg. We headed southwestward, directly before the wind. It wasn't long before we realized that the great ship with its vast spread of canvas, able to carry more sail than we in this sea and wind because she was more boat also, was overtaking us. About this time we looked back and saw two puffs of smoke over her bow, followed by a flash of fire. Several seconds later the boom of these guns came across the ocean separating us. Two great black balls flew through the air and landed on either side of our little ship, short of the stern, thank God! We were still out of range!

All agreed the situation was serious; no one was smiling now. Our captain ordered us to sail off on the quarter and thus increase our speed. He also knew it would take them much longer to correct the vast number of sails they were carrying. We quickly trimmed in, sailed off on the quarter, and it increased our speed greatly. As a result, the next two shots fired from their bow guns landed further astern. The captain then called Mr. Sykes and Mr. Pearsall to his side, beckoned to Mr. Purchase and Henry Springer, and a conference followed. It was decided that we would try to keep out of range of this ship, but lead her on toward Little Egg, if possible. I thought, why should a great ship, a great merchantman, or perhaps a transport, chase a little ship? Unless she recognized us, knowing our name and reputation.

All through the day we headed in the general direction of Little Egg. We sailed on the quarter in order to keep our distance. But she came on and on. The wind was increasing in violence all the time. The seas were large, steep and close together, their troughs narrow and deep. The ocean was a boiling caldron of angry water. The long, high ground swells looked more like great moving mountains of water racing along with us. The sky was now more overcast. The great ship was determined to catch us or drive us on the beach. She was certain that we could not elude her by passing through any inlet on the coast in this sea. She knew she could outrun us as the seas increased in violence and the wind increased in velocity.

From time to time there were more snow flurries. We altered our course again, running on the quarter on the other tack. We now headed a true course for Little Egg. She corrected her course, cutting off some of the distance which was consumed by our turn, and presently she began to fire again. Again the shots landed on either side of our little ship. The situation was bad. The bow watch called back and pointed to the shore. It was late afternoon now. We could see the evergreen forests along the beach. With the glass, I could see the inlet of Little Egg. The inlet was a boiling mountain of white water rushing for the shore. I saw the houses on Tucker Island to the north of the inlet, so comfortable and secure. It didn't seem possible that such comfort could be such a short distance away. We had to get through the inlet. How close to shore would this great ship come before she gave up the chase? The wind was playing a melancholy dirge through our rigging. Was this it? Was this to be our end?

*168*

The sky was rapidly becoming darker and the sea an ominous gray. Perhaps due to the shoaling of the water, the seas were much steeper. Darkness was closing in and the lights were coming on in the houses on Tucker Beach. The boom of the surf could be heard ahead. It was snowing again. We were roaring along, partly due to the gale force of the wind, partly due to the howling seas. We looked ahead in the semidarkness. We could see a light flashing on and off, on and off, just to the south of the inlet.

"My God!" the captain exclaimed. "The Barnegat Pirates are at work!"

The crash of the surf on the beach could be heard above the roaring of the waves and the whistling of the wind. Mr. Cook, with his hawk-eyes, was sent to the bow. I was stationed midships to call back information from Mr. Cook. We were going through this inlet in the dark. We had to make it. Our only markers on the north were the lights in the houses; our marker on the south was this bonfire on the beach, with the horse or mule wearing a long blanket, walking round and round, giving the impression of a light flashing on and off in a lighthouse. Our markers straight ahead were the lights in the houses in Tuckerton. Good Lord, please help us make it. We sailed on and Mr. Cook called back time and time again, "Clear water ahead! No breakers!" I repeated the call to the captain, who stood tensely beside the wheel, for the first time his mouth was drawn tight as a kettledrum head. Mr. Sykes and Mr. Pearsall stood at the wheel. The captain now moved to the rail and watched the water as it rushed by, trying to determine its depth. We could hear the incessant boom of the guns on the big ship, in spite of the howling gale, but we could no longer see the flashes. Two more booms followed and then a crash! The balls struck us in the stern counter. The little vessel shuddered. I was ordered to go below to ascertain the damage. Mr. Irons replaced me midships to call back the news from Mr. Cook to the captain.

The galley was a shambles. There was a hole right through where the stern window had been. Our beautiful brass gun was unmounted and thrown aside. The fine Wedgewood crockery which had been presented to the captain when the *Blazing Star* went into commission, was in a thousand pieces. Then I saw Richard. He was pinned under the great brass gun, bleeding from a hundred wounds. Death was close at hand. I had never seen it close up before, but I recognized it anyway. I rushed up to the captain and he came down at once. He wanted to say something cheerful, so he said, "Richard, why didn't you catch that cannon ball?" Poor Richard looked up with a half faint smile and said, "Master, even da cannonball got to have room." He closed his eyes. In the flickering candlelight, I saw the purple, then the blue color pass over his dark lips, like a moving shadow. And then he was gone.

The captain quickly ascended the stairs. Mr. Springer and Mr. Purchase were sent down to make emergency repairs and to get Richard out. These repairs were necessary if the breakers were to be kept out and if we were going to successfully traverse the inlet. We had at least a mile of breakers ahead.

It was almost dark now and we could no longer see the great ship. The snow was whirling. The mates and the captain seemed satisfied with their course, and we sailed on. Now we were parallel on our right with the lights in the houses on Tucker Island and the false light high on the sand dunes on the south side of the inlet, the light from the huge bonfire.

Suddenly there was a lurch and we stopped. Masses of angry water rushed by and a great sea passed entirely over us. The spray reached the masthead. We had struck the bar. The next sea lifted us and we sailed on. Suddenly we struck again and harder. I thought from the abrupt stop and the violence of the wind that we would be dismasted. Two seas crashed up on the counter, partly passed over us, and the spray ascended again to the top of our rigging. How could men make a repair against such an avalanche of water. We lifted and moved on again, this time more sluggishly than before. Mr. Purchase and Mr. Springer ascended the companionway stairs carrying Richard. They were tired, wet, cold, and half drowned. They said, "We've got at least three feet of water in the hold, Captain."

They agreed that we had probably knocked part of her keel off and broken her back. What could keep us afloat? If we could just reach Tuckertown. We were inside the inlet now, sailing slowly and sluggishly in fairly calm water. We threw the cannons over the side, but our little ship was dying and we all knew it. All the spared men were devoted to the pumps and I was sent below to measure the water. There was definitely three feet of water in the hold. The water was sloshing back and forth in the chart room. Poor Richard, who hated the sea, dead! He only went to sea because he loved us all. This was Richard's brave end! The middle hatch was open and some of the men began bailing with buckets. As I stood in the darkness, except for the flicker of a candle lantern, I could see the water rising. I called up and told the captain. I looked out the companionway. The snow had stopped; the stars were out; the night was cold and clear, and the wind had lessened. The creek lay ahead! In five minutes we would be in the creek.

We suddenly heard the boom of guns. We looked back toward the inlet and saw rockets going into the air—distress rockets. That great ship, thinking we were going in through Sandy Hook Inlet, had been deceived by the Barnegat Pirates. She was doomed. In a matter of minutes she would be a total wreck. The beach fire was now blazing, no longer in imitation of a lighthouse. Undoubtedly, the fiends were already celebrating their prize.

We reached Parker's Creek. Then suddenly we stopped. We were aground now, on the bottom. I looked out into the darkness. The stars were twinkling in the clear night sky and I could see the willow trees on the bank, the same willow trees we had tied to in the hurricane. It was here that our good ship died.

The captain went below, waist-deep in the icy water, picked up the log book from the top of the cabinet and brought it up, together with the ship's money. Nothing further was said. We lowered the long boat, put Richard in the bottom, and rowed up the creek to Parkerstown.

When we entered the inn, the captain walked to the desk

and told the innkeeper that there was a great British ship on the beach at the inlet and that help should be sent immediately.

"Since it's a British ship, that's their lookout!" he replied.

Our captain then told him that the Barnegat Pirates were at work again; this was an opportunity to catch them if we could round up enough men in the town. I don't remember the innkeeper's reply, but whatever it was, it indicated clearly in my mind, and certainly in the minds of the crew, that this man was part and parcel of the Barnegat Pirates.

There was nothing further we could do, so we ate our supper and went to bed. As I lay there, I thought of the increased prosperity of this inn in the past three years. It had been a plain, comfortable inn before, just a coach stop. After the sacking of Little Egg, Parkerstown had developed into a very prosperous community. Now this inn was as beautifully furnished and as richly adorned with fine things as any of the finest inns in the world, said our captain. The walls and woodwork were decorated in rich colors, the damask draperies were a cardinal red with threads of gold woven through in a Chinese effect. The furniture consisted of fine, selected pieces of the period, and the pewter, the silver, the plate, and the flatware showed by their crests, and insignias that they had most certainly come from many great ships.

The next morning was very clear, but cold. We got up early, buried Richard in the Quaker cemetery, and paid for his marker. Then we went down to view our little ship, this time in a large wagon. Her deck was awash and her sails were tattered and torn, but flaunting in the wind as so many holiday pennants. There was nothing we could do about her. Mr. Springer and Mr. Purchase had agreed that her bottom was practically gone. How she had ever made the creek was more than we could understand, unless that was where she wanted to die. As I looked at her, I thanked the good Lord for our deliverance and my many blessings.

We looked across the bay to the inlet. Sure enough, there stood the great British transport, almost high and dry in the inlet.

We returned to town; we hoisted the sail on our long boat. And on that cold December morning, we sailed across to the south beach at the inlet. As we came ashore and walked across the beach, we saw a long boat floating and rocking peacefully in a little lagoon left by the tide. A British soldier's body was draped over the side, a bullet wound through his chest. We walked down along the beach and there at the edge of the surf we saw a great number of bodies—of English ladies in their laces and finery, many of them with their bonnets still tied to their heads. Their wet clothing was draped close to their bodies, almost as the partially draped statues of ancient Greek women. Even in death, they were very beautiful, and there was a certain stoicism in their masklike features. In their early training as ladies, they had been taught to meet any eventuality with calm aloofness and courage.

Intermingled with them, and often side by side, were other women with cheaper clothing. They were generally fat and bloated in appearance, and their faces bore the look of dissipation. It was evident that this was a British transport coming to New York with the ladies to visit their husbands at Christmas, and the harlots for the British troops.

As the waves rolled back and forth at low tide, the bodies would sway back and forth, the arms moving in rhythm and the dresses fluttering. The captain pointed out the hands that had been chopped off at the wrist in the haste to remove bracelets and the fingers cut off to remove rings.

There were many men, sailors and marines lying dead along the beach. There were others who had apparently come ashore in one of the long boats and had survived, only to be subsequently murdered, for their bodies lay along the beach, some at the surf's edge and some on higher ground.

Presently we came to a group of women high behind a sand dune. Their fingers had been chopped off and their throats slit, and by the condition of their clothing, we knew they had been assaulted. The embers were still glowing in this huge fire of deception, and there was a deep circular track about the fire made by the horse or mule, just as our captain had described.

We buried these unfortunate people on high ground, marking their graves by turning the long boat over on top of it. Then we carved the date on the hull with our knives, adding the particulars. The name of the great ship was on the stern of the long boat. This was a suitable marker. The name read *The Royal Scot.* We returned to our boat sadly and sailed across Little Egg Bay and on to Parkerstown.

The mounted militia was just returning from across the state, but they had come too late. When we told their captain what had happened, he said, "The sons of bitches! And to think I got here just a little too late! But we may catch them yet! The only road from the south beach joins this road about 15 miles in. What are you going to do now?"

"We're going home."

"Oh, have you heard the news? The war is over!"

"My great God!" cried the captain. "Had we only known this, we could have prevented this frightful disaster."

We had saved nothing except the ship's log, my diary, the ship's money, the bow swivel, and the clothing on our backs. Since the stage was leaving with the militia, we all took one last longing look at the little ship lying far away in the creek, its tattered sails as so many hands waving a final good-bye. The coach lurched to a start and we looked away, glad to leave Parkerstown.

We were all very sad as we passed along the road through the Pine Barrens. No one spoke. A little before noon the mounted militia left us and galloped ahead at great speed. We loaded our pistols and held them ready for firing, more than a little concerned. Why had the militia left us at a time like this, right in the danger area?

As we rode up a little hill on the road, we saw just ahead a caravan entirely surrounded by our mounted militia.* It

---

*Led by Major Lawrence Stratton of Bridgeton

had just come onto our road from a road to the south. We realized that this must be the road that led across the great marsh from the south side of the inlet. Here was the caravan of the Pine Barons, the Pine Robbers, and the Barnegat Pirates, caught dead to rights. Five had already confessed and were now accusing the others. The leaders in particular protested their innocence of any wrongdoing—except robbing the dead. They claimed that everyone was dead when they came ashore to which our captain exclaimed, "Do you assault dead women?"

The leaders hung their heads and said, "No." That clinched it! Three men had escaped into the swamp. The captain of the militia was calling into the swamp giving them a last warning to return or he would set fire to it. Presently they came out through the deep grass, nearly frozen and wet almost to their waists. They, too, began to accuse the leaders, as the rest had been doing. They were all clapped into irons. Although we wanted to hang them right then and there, they were taken ahead to Trenton, imprisoned, and finally hung.*

We proceeded on to Mt. Holly, where we caught the stage going through to (Freehold) Monmouth Court House. We left the militia, having thanked them for their great aid throughout the trying years. We promised that when we were needed as witnesses, we would appear before the court at Trenton to give testimony. This was not necessary, however, for twelve of the cowards turned State's evidence and made a clean breast of their depredations throughout the war.

At Freehold, Mr. Purchase, Mr. Hance, Mr. Irons, and Mr. Orange shook hands all around and said good-bye. We promised to meet once a year, at Christmas time, at the old farm house on the edge of Amboy, and we always did.

We rested at Freehold overnight at Augie Desner's Inn, having arrived late in the evening. The next day we took the stage and passed on to Middletown Point, very anxious

---

*Records in the Trenton Hall of Archives

*175*

to get home now. We hired a large farm wagon, paying the farmer handsomely, and he took us through to the south side of Raritan River, where we obtained a ferry and crossed to Amboy. Friends picked us up there in a number of carriages and carried us up to the farm. We arrived there after dark on a cold day in December, just before Christmas.

As we walked up to the door of the farm house, I recall that everything seemed just as we had left it. As I looked through the window, tears filled my eyes. There was my little boy playing on the floor. We rapped on the door, then pushed it open and walked in.

There were yells, cries and tears followed by much caressing. I think all the members of the crew who were there received as many embraces as I did.

I grabbed my wife and my little boy, then closed my eyes and just stood there, overcome with emotion. The little fellow had never seen me, yet somehow he seemed to know who I was. He clung to my legs as my wife and I moved over to the fire, sat down on the floor, and just looked at each other.

The slaves now freemen stood in the doorway grinning. The evening was a series of homecomings. Slaves soon came in from the rest of the farm and people came in from town. It was well past midnight before the last light was blown out.

We were home—home to stay. Everything would have been perfect had the little *Blazing Star* been rocking at anchor in the little creek at the back of the farm. But in quieter moments, in reflection, my father and I agreed that it was fitting that *Blazing Star* should end her days in Parker's Creek at Little Egg, the port from which she had done such gallant work throughout the American Revolution. There she stood, a monument to the things for which individual American seafaring men stand. And as her mast stood for years, towering toward the sky, she remained a symbol of the height to which Americans will rise in any emergency.

# NOTES

1. Major Charles William Gilman, M.D., Commander Jersey Blues.
2. The ships out of Bristol, England were considered the best kept ships in the world.
3. The British came the next day, seized 24 Sagg Harbour and East Hampton men, cast them into prison in the Old Sugar House, a New York warehouse and, without trial, later transferred them to the Jersey, the infamous prison ship.
4. Also called a Kentucky rifle; first made in Lancaster County, Pennsylvania. Patterned somewhat after the German Jaeger or hunting musket and the 1763 Charlesville, but with a long barrel and a much improved lock. Subsequently carried down the long valley to the Kentucky Frontier and later made there also.
5. To holystone a deck is to take a holystone, a soft type of limestone, throw salt water in quantities on the deck, and get down on hands and knees and rub back and forth. After much effort, time, and subsequent stiffness, the pine deck becomes a bleached white. The chlorine in the water is released by the sandstone and does the bleaching. The white planks, with the black tar between, makes a deck look very Bristol fashion.
6. At the beginning of the embargo, the British placed restrictions on firearms and locks. Many locks and barrels were smuggled in but there was still a great shortage. The various committees of safety thus ordered the making of arms by several hundred local gunsmiths. Many of these men became very famous and the guns became known as Committee of Safety muskets.
7. Excluding the mates and captain.
8. Staten Island remained a British port throughout the war.
9. The same old herring that Washington wanted to be king.
10. See Mellick, Andrew D. The Story of an old Farm.
11. Begun in 1775; finished in 1802.
12. Hot shot required no fuse or torch to the touchhole. Shot was heated to a glow, dumped into the muzzle from the ladle, and contact with the powder caused instantaneous fire. Of course, the loaders had to be quick in stepping back for the risk was great.
13. Fire rails were placed along the rails at weak points, where boarding usually occurred. If a torch was touched to the long pan, the short barrelled blunderbuss guns, filled with shot, nails, chips of iron, broken glass, and even crockery, would go off like a machine gun as the fire traveled along the pan.

# BIBLIOGRAPHY

### Books and Records

Bancroft, George. *History of the United States* (First Edition).
Barber and Howe. *New Jersey Historical Collections.*
Blackman, Leah. *History of Little Egg Harbor Township.*
Boudinot, Elias. *Boudinot's Journal.*
Chastelleaux. *Voyage in America.*
Dally, Rev. Joseph W. *The Story of a New Jersey Town.* Woodbridge.
Force, Peter (Lord Mahon). *History of the American Declaration of Independence.*
Franklin, Benjamin. *The Farmer's Letters.* 1767.
Gilman, Drake, Hunter, Thoms families. *Bible* records.
Hopkins, Alfred E. *Weapons and Equipment of Early American Soldiers.*
United States Department of the Interior. Library of Congress. *American Privateer.*
Manucy, Albert. *Artillery Throughout the Ages.*
Mellick, Andrew D. *The Story of an Old Farm.*
Monnette, Orra Eugene. *Ye Early History of Woodbridge and Piscataway.* (7 volumes)
Newark, N.J. *Records of the New Jersey Historical Society.*
New Jersey Historical Society. *Proceedings.*
New London Historical Society. *Proceedings.*
New York. Museum of the City of New York. *Little Old New York.*
Pennypacker, Morton. *Historical Collections of East Hampton.*
Perth Amboy. *Records of St. Peter's Church.*
Piscataway, N.J. Tombstone records and records of the Episcopal Church.
Rahway, N.J. *Records.*
Rutgers University. Historical Society Collection of New Jersey. *General Stryker's Colonial Troops of the New Jersey Line.*
Salter and Beekman. *Old Times in Old Monmouth* (very rare).
Sons of the American Revolution. Records of the Sons of the American Revolution Library, Elizabeth, N.J.

Sparks, Jed. *Benjamin Franklin.*
Sparks, Jed. *Washington's Correspondence.*
Washington, D.C. National Archives. *Botta's History of our War of Independence,* written and translated into English.
Woodbridge, N.J. The records of the Old First Presbyterian Church, Liber I, II, III. Tombstone records.
Woodbridge, N.J. Records and town meetings 1669-1900.
Woodbridge, N.J. Town meeting records of Woodbridge and Piscataway, 1636-1846, from the vault of the Town Hall of Woodbridge.
Van Doren, Carl. *Secret Correspondence of the American Revolution.*
Whitehead. *Contributions to East Jersey History.*
Yeoman, Dr. *Correlation and Conservation of Forces.*

### Articles

Hamilton, Alexander. *The Continentalist.* New York Astor Library, 1774, 1775 and 1781.
Hartford, Conn. State House. *Connecticut in the Revolution.*
Paine, Tom. *Common Sense.* New York Astor Library.

### Newspaper Files from the Revolutionary Period at:

| | |
|---|---|
| New Brunswick | White Plains |
| Piscataway | Tarrytown |
| Woodbridge | Peekskill |
| Perth Amboy | Newburg |
| Rahway | Albany |
| Elizabeth | Schoharie |
| Newark | Kingston |
| Westfield | Brooklyn |
| Morristown | New York City: |
| Trenton | Astor Library |
| Rutgers Hall of Archives | Columbiana Collection, |
| Princeton University Library | Library of Columbia U. |